T0147196

BLAZING LIGHT
. . . In the Grace of One Journey

EMELY BATIN–ORILLOS

authorHOUSE®

AuthorHouse™
1663 Liberty Drive
Bloomington, IN 47403
www.authorhouse.com
Phone: 1 (800) 839-8640

© 2019 EMELY BATIN–ORILLOS. All rights reserved.

No part of this book may be reproduced, stored in a retrieval system, or transmitted by any means without the written permission of the author.

Published by AuthorHouse 05/07/2019

ISBN: 978-1-7283-1054-1 (sc)
ISBN: 978-1-7283-1056-5 (e)

Print information available on the last page.

Any people depicted in stock imagery provided by Getty Images are models, and such images are being used for illustrative purposes only. Certain stock imagery © Getty Images.

This book is printed on acid-free paper.

Because of the dynamic nature of the Internet, any web addresses or links contained in this book may have changed since publication and may no longer be valid. The views expressed in this work are solely those of the author and do not necessarily reflect the views of the publisher, and the publisher hereby disclaims any responsibility for them.

Scripture taken from The Holy Bible, King James Version. Public Domain

FOREWORD

Eduardo R. Alicias Jr. He is a man of grit, integrity. He is a man who lives between gravity and levity. In moments of gravity, he means what he says—with grit. He has this essential trait that if he thinks he is right, most likely he is; and should there be a counter-argument, most likely he would prevail on grounds of syllogistic or deductive validity and empirical soundness, meaning that what he is saying corresponds with or approximates actual or factual verity. Oh, he cerebrates much like his idol-epistemologist, Karl Popper, earlier did with his quest for the "verisimilitude". He is well grounded on bits and pieces of information of whatever sort, inasmuch as he is voracious, i.e., epistemically ravenous in all aspects of nature—ranging from, say, the infinite gravity and singularity of a cosmologic black hole to the infinite attractiveness of a pinkly hole, of paradisiac cul-de-sac the presence and essence of which is advertised by the blackey grass-like salience of ambient mons pubis or mons veneris. However, he is all too willing to accept his mistakes and in all humility in the rare instances they do occur.

He is passionate in what he believes in. He moves heaven and earth, so to speak, to convince you of his belief, of his position, of his arguments--giving emphasis on the showing of evidence cum the force of deductive and syllogistic reasoning. He rarely raises his voice in anger to convince you;

he listens to your arguments. However, in the end, if you remain unconvinced, still he respects you and your opinion. His being passionate is evident in his writings. Also, when he starts writing, you can expect him to finish the article/book within his scheduled timetable.

He is a gentleman. Over the years I have seen, I have been a lucky personal witness of his intellectual passion and capability. But, he does not brag about it nor does he take pleasure in criticizing the deficiency or weaknesses of others. He is so unassuming; he appears so ordinary ["manong", "lolo" or "uncle"], but when you look at his achievements and his writings, oh, such genius!

"Manong" as I fondly call him is not perfect. But as a mortal, he is exceptional, a *rara avis*! Indeed, I'm lucky to have been his student and dissertation adviser at the University of the Philippines, Diliman. I'm lucky to have been his Associate Editor when he was the Editor of **THE SEARCH JOURNAL**, ISSN 0117-6439. I'm lucky to have been his "Ading" all these years.

DR. JULIET A. CATANE
Dean, College of Liberal Arts
Technological University of the Philippines

"OH GOD, MY HEART IS FIXED;
I WILL SING AND GIVE PRAISE,
EVEN WITH MY GLORY."
[PSALM 108:1]

"YES, I'M ALL TOO HUMAN.
MY IDOL IS ST. AUGUSTINE OF HIPPO
WHO SAID: "LORD, PLEASE
MAKE ME A SAINT
BUT NOT YET."
-EDUARDO R. ALICIAS JR.

APERITIF

ALICIAS, JR., E.

IS TOO SEXY

FOR MY PEN!

"UNTO THE UPRIGHT
THERE ARISETH LIGHT
IN THE DARKNESS..."
[PSALM 112:4]

ACKNOWLEDGMENT

Another wonderful miracle in my life! This biography of a 73-year old man of revolutionary science, quixotic art, and exuberant humor I would not have written with my lowly little pen had he chosen to compose the longest of more of his longest, instead, but he trusted my grief, my sorrow, and my tears to chronicle his life's a million and one moments in the sun, as well as his wanton hours in the pits and dungeons of darkness, human wretchedness, lust, obsession, pride, and prejudice. I say THANK YOU TO MY FORMER UP PROFESSOR, DR. EDUARDO R. ALICIAS, JR., for the trust and confidence! While my late husband's tragic death from the hands of medical malpractitioners almost always sends me to my own abyss of nothingness since APRIL 11, 2017, the moment my little pen began scribbling the words to tell the life story of the FILIPINO GENIUS who has a GUINNESS WORLD RECORD recognition, among his other fabulous achievements, my tears have been falling and rolling, with laughter in between, for the man's humor is inevitably bombastic and explosive, leaving not even a single stone unturned. My lowly pen is more than graciously, gratefully, and fortunately honoured and privileged.

Likewise, to all of those who generously shared their recollections of the young Eduardo, the middle-aged

EDUARDO, and the great gray Eduardo. To Atty. Felix Racadio, Dr. Gerry Toentino, Dr. Ferdinand Lamarca, Dean Dr. Juliet Catane, Dr. Danny Hilario, Prof. Aurelio P. Ramos Jr., Prof. Francis Alfaro, Prof. Al Cao, and Dr. Cecille Velasco, I am more than grateful. You are truly the finest men and women who sat in the classes of the great teacher! MABUHAY PO KAYONG LAHAT! But, my little, lowly pen would never have learned to work with words had my parents, TEOFILO SABALBURO AND LOURDES PIMENTEL BATIN, not raised me in a home that was warm and loving, disciplined and encouraging, with lots of story-telling, singing, and dancing, of course, a home with God as its center and essence of being. Had my parents not built our house in the heart of wonderful uncorrupted nature, and had they not bought me rims and rims of bond papers, and had not my father bought us a large dictionary, and had he not subscribed for me regular monthly editions of READER'S DIGEST, that little Indian war girl would not have been inspired to look into, and appreciate the beauty of life, in all of its splendour and horror. THANK YOU, Papang and Mamang! I will always be grateful for raising me in the sunshine, and well, the rainy days of life. Of course, I would never have learned to pray with my heart, and sleep not with fairy tales if our grandmother, ALEJANDRA TEJADA-PIMENTEL chose to just smoke her Virginia *tabaco*, drink her *Sioktong*, and sell her ILOCOS *ules* as far as her purse and strength could take her. What can I say to all my siblings but thank you as well for all the fun and sweet adventures we had together while growing up, like swimming in the BANAOANG/ABRA RIVER, *Paraiso ni Juan*, climbing all the Mango and *Sarguelas* trees, including the cherries and the berries, and the endless running in open fields. I am as grateful for all those beautiful, fun memories of childhood to you, my siblings: ELOIDA, ELREY, ERLEEN, ELY, ESTELA MARIE, ERROL ANTHONY, AND

ETHEL CONSUELO; Thank you also to our stepmother, Chelly Bello, the rest of our family [Lino, Grace, Boy, Guiller, Armee, Emilson, Marilou, Luz, Cathy, Digna, Sunshine, Aries, Earl, Lorraine, Miki, Lyndon, Diana, Caesar, Lyka, Roman, Maja Mae, Laarni Rose, Alyssa Lourdes, Ivan, Niko, Lyra, Ella, Marcial, Jepong, Mark, Allan, Maureen, Lanz, Hurley, And All The Little Ones; The Late Lolo Baak Tejada, Lola Enriqueta Tejada, Lolo Sixto Batin, Lola Augusta Batin, Auntie Nelly Tejada, Auntie Ilay Batin, Lolo Rafael Pimentel, Lolo Juaning Tejada, Auntie Sonia Tejada, And My Dearest Uncle Roland Del Castillo Tejada; my good friends: Jayne Velasco-Blanco, Nerisse Bundoc-Dizon, Edith Tolentino-Birosel, Gina Jalandoni, Janet, Rey Cabalo, Albert Oasan, Ponce Carreon, Merceditas Alcantara, Laarni Parayno, Chito San Mateo, Edwin Martin, Fr. Bien Miguel, Jun Caubalejo, Fely And Mina, Alex Puente, Charlie Veric, Cori Quitoriano-Perez, Florian Sideco, John Tigno, Danton Remoto, Lally Nillo-Prado, Christy Sajor, Susanna Dycheepuat-Go, Cheryl Gonzales-Pineda, Tony Tuviera, Neil Satokya, Paul Poblete, Edeliza Tacata, Teresa Formozo-Pescador, Caridad Singson, Ruby Zablan, Wendy Reyes, Janet Mabalo, Minerva Mosca, Mina Cumuyog, Rose Neri, Nids Ilago, Araceli Fernando, Candy Remigio, Fideliz Tuy, Estrellita Madriaga, Cadz Malbaroza, Feorillo Demeterio, The Late Vicky Carbonnel; All my childhood friends especially May Brilliantes-Panganiban, Sandra Corpuz, Hilda Bosque-Ice, Erlinda Villanueva, Marilyn Buenavista, Cora Sarmiento, Nestor De Peralta, Herbert "Silver" De Peralta, Calixto Cardenas, Constante Garcia, Pablito Martinez, Atong Bielza, Joseph Benaza; Our Dear Ninang Nonette Corpuz, Marlu Vilches, Lulu Reyes, Shayne Lumbera, April Fernandez, Auntie Purita Tejada, Auntie Tessie Tejada, Auntie Sally Tejada, Auntie Evelyn Tejada, Auntie Maribel Tejada; All My Cousins Especially Judith Batin, Angel Martinez, And Santiago Martinez, Dr. Fe Nava, Our Ever So

Kind Pediatrician, Dra. Anna Bautista-La Vega, Flor Cacapit, Kring Fontejon, Atty. Sol Lumba, Atty. Arpee And Nina Alentajan, Havanna Guillermo, And Of course, The good SPC nuns especially Sr. Mary Celine Santos, SPC; Sr. Nilda Hechanova, RA, Sr. Henrietta Gomez, Sr. Tine Bajarin, Sr. Consuelo Albino, RVM, And The Wonderful Priests Of God: FR. UBALDUS DJONDA, SVD [Thank you po, Fr. Uz For Buying Me My New Microsoft Office!], Fr. Leonard Rosario Shankar, Fr. Roy Matthew, Fr. George Rosario, Fr. Manny Flores, SJ; All my loyal graduate students especially Danny Balance, Ramil Pellogo, Miguel Lorenzo Garcia, Jo Alarcon, Michelle Desierto, Elisa Ang, Fleurdeliz Parulan, Virginia Sembrano, Jenny Roco, Virna Villanueva, Consuelo Gregorio, Cristeta Tapia, Helen, Angelo Glori, James, Jc Castro, Angelo Sicat, Joselito Alipio, Jerry Bang-As, Aj Jacobe, Paolo Carlo Victoria, Patrick Genove, John Paul Bartolome, Bitwin Ayalin, Eden Avila, Helen Madrigal, Diana Dela Cruz, Violeta Gajudo, Anna Manabat, Carmela Raguine, Mildred Danao, Angel Balte. To everyone who has inspired me to face the world again and write for GOD'S GREATER GLORY, MARAMING SALAMAT PO! But this heart keeps beating because of my one and only son, JOSEPH MARY PETER PAUL LAMB LORENZO ANSELMO MARY THE BLESSED "JP", and the beautiful memories of my beloved, LORENZO QUIAMBAO ORILLOS [I love you forever Papa!]. Not to forget our little zoo, our sweet legendary menagerie that helps me keep my head and bear my pain! MAMA MARY, PAPA JOSEPH, GOD THE FATHER AND THE HOLY SPIRIT, I offer this gift of love and sacrifice, and thank you for your constant guidance and divine inspiration. TO THE MAN ON THE CROSS, I LOVE YOU, and thank you for consoling me and my child! AUTHORHOUSE, United States, **AGYAMANAK! MARAMING SALAMAT PO! TO GOD BE THE GLORY**!

INTRODUCTION

**The Glory that is EDUARDO
REZONABLE ALICIAS JR.
The Grandeur that is EDUARDO
REZONABLE ALICIAS JR.
HE WHO HOLDS AND WIELDS
"ERIMAKO'S PEN"!**

Thirty-five years ago, I sat trembling in his class with my left-foot red and right foot pink ribbon*ed* dainty socks on a still spotless pair of white TRETORN sneakers while my bright red-laced blouse and black cotton double-pocket mini skirt were more shy than my unkempt perfectly innocent eyebrows. He was my first ever professor in my graduate studies at the University of the Philippines in Diliman. The course was Education and National Development. I was twenty years old. He was thirty-nine, and oh, he sent my jitters away after ten to fifteen minutes of his lecture on eggplants, inflation, quality and cost of education, and sex education! I sighed in relief as I thought I was to learn more of classical reverence for exorbitant classical thought though I loved classical poetry or its folly. Even now!

He talked sexy, he computed sexy, he thought sexy!

Undeniably, he's a man, inarguably of corporal, corporeal entity, inarguably brilliant, a genius of flesh and mind, a master of both matter and no-matter, simply no matter.

My youth was seduced, tantalized more than corrupted. I started to question more persistently my own essence, my own purpose, my own universe, including, oh, the educational leadership of my school principal, though I was just beginning as well to teach as an English and Journalism High School teacher at St. Mary's College, Quezon City.

Unfortunately, my intellect was too feeble compared to the veteran and alert minds of my much older classmates though there was Rommel, an instructor then of Physical Education, also in UPD who was just three years older than my birth certificate, and he would listen patiently to me when I reported my poor research on the maladies and illnesses of Philippine education [I read all three volumes of Renato Constantino's "Issues Without Tears"!], while my brilliant professor and my advance learners of classmates [like Bro. Manny De Leon of Marist School, *Ate* Teresita Anastacio of Claret School, the Palawan oil exploration pilot, Herman Mapua; businessman Yap from Davao, a Malacañang Palace Colonel, and Fr. Ding of Don Bosco Pampanga]were busy deciphering the mystery of the BAMBOO ORGAN in Las Piñas, and how this masterpiece of local ingenuity could be an inspiration for a more relevant contemporary Filipino education]. At the end of my first academic semester in the country's premier state university, the man of infinite REGRESSION ANALYSIS and untrammelled humor decided to give me the lowest grade of 1.75, almost a failing grade in the master's program, to his class of about twenty-five professionals. Of course, I was also the least professional as I just stepped out of a royal, pontifical university, with no yet college diploma, transcript of records, and work experience when I enrolled in the Master of Education in Educational Administration Program in UP, together with my sweet good *tsinoy* friend, Susanna Dycheepuat, who enrolled at the Department of Educational Foundations, and whose younger sister, a maroon undergrad, shouldered the three hundred pesos I lacked for my tuition. But, I was more than elated for I survived the exquisite yet cryptic intellect and genius of DR. EDUARDO R. ALICIAS JR.

The two decades and many more years that followed saw the controversial rise and fall, trial and victory, sin and redemption of a great man. Almost metaphorical to Shelley's "OZYMANDIAS," quite allegorical to Moses, evidently gravitational to Einstein! As for the feeble-minded student, she went through the labyrinths, the tunnels, and the catacombs of searchings and wailings.

Until OCTOBER 2018.

The path of the once trembling, obstinate fool of a twenty year-old student, with now some FOUR NEURONS [thanks Joemar Lazaro Furigay!] in her head, crossed again with the blazing path of a rare FILIPINO GENIUS, who wrote two of the world's most extraordinarily crafted books of all time, BREAKING RECORDS! These two magnum opuses, he wrote them in an interval of historic twelve years. His "HUMOR AND MADNESS"[1997] was recognized by the GUINNESS WORLD RECORDS organization [GWR] as having the LONGEST PREFACE ever written relative to the main body of the book. Its sequel, "HUMOR AND MADNESS, JR." [2009], arguably has the longest preface ever written in absolute length, consisting of only ONE SENTENCE in 62,705 words; this lexico-syntactico brilliantly fascinating superb creation is "arguably, the THIRD LONGEST ENGLISH SENTENCE EVER WRITTEN!" And his poem, "ERIMAKO'S PEN" is internationally acclaimed [published in **RAINSTORMS AND RAINBOWS**, c2000, an anthology published by the International Library of Poetry [ILP 2000, Owings Mills, MD, USA], which earned for him DISTINGUISHED

HONORARY MEMBERSHIP in the International Poets Society; and the same is also published in **2001-A POETIC ODYSSEY**, c2001; Famous Poets Society, Talent, Oregon, USA. Likewise, his poem "I Made a Mistake" [attack versus the pharisaical establishment] is included in **TAKING FLIGHT**, c2001, an anthology published by the International Library of Poetry [ILP], 2001, Owings Mills, MD, USA. Moreover, he and his poem, "Beyond Contiguity"[catharsis for unconsummated love]are included and/or published in THE BEST POEMS & POETS of 2001, c2002, International Library of Poetry, Owings Mills, MD, USA.

Life might not have been as picturesque but the controversial odyssey of the Philippine ULYSSES gave birth to a lot more of great works. Today, the great thinker of his own rank and class has written a string of fabulous books. His authorship is nonetheless rarefied. Oh God, he gave me nine of his THIRTEEN magnum opera that he expects me [perhaps!] to read and decode them with how he wrote and encoded them! Jesus! Nevertheless, when I get more neurons, I will read all these books:

1. Data Organization and Analysis in a Computer Environment, c1995 & c1997, ISBN 971-91402-08;

2. Classroom Observation and Related Fallacies: Lessons for Educational Administration, c1996, ISBN 971-91402-1-6;

3. Humor and Madness, c1997, ISBN 971-91402-3-2, GWR!;

4. Forms of Government and the Occurrence of Coups D' Etat, c2007, Trafford Publishing, Victoria, BC, Canada; c2009, Philippine Edition;

5. Humor and Madness, Jr., c2009, 1997, ISBN 971-91402-3-2;

6. Parliamentarism and Other Ways to National Wealth and Welfare, c2012, published by Amazon/Kindle as ebook;

7. Homicide and Other Violent Crimes: The Folly of the Gun Ban, c2013, published by Amazon/Kindle as ebook;

8. Poems Past Noontide: 11th Hour Madness [co-authored with Ladie Dee, 3 March 2014], published by Amazon/Kindle as ebook;

9. The Underlying Science, The Utility of Acquiring Early English Proficiency: The Flawed Mother Tongue Based Multilingual Education [MTBMLE] Policy, c2014, ISBN 978-971-011-903-5, Central Book Supply, Inc.; Quezon City, Philippines;

10. Notes on the History and Philosophy of Scientific Inquiry, First Edition, c2017, published by Loyola Heights Student Center (Aurelio P. Ramos Jr.), Loyola Heights, Quezon City:

11. Ejaculates From The Heart, c2018, Erimako, A. [his nom de plume] and S. H. Valdez; Vigan, Ilocos Sur, Philippines;

12. Evaluating Government Structures and Policies: The Factual Versus Counterfactual, c2017; Loyola Heights Student Center (Aurelio P. Ramos Jr.), ISBN 978-971-9912-03-3;

13. The Epigone's Two Cents Versus the Beacon's Five Cents, c2019, Central Book Supply, Inc., Quezon City, ISBN 978-621-02-0655-5.

But, his most unique, significant, revolutionary contribution to education research, the pioneering Variance Partitioning Analysis [VPA] model, comes in an article he titled, **"Toward an Objective Evaluation of Teacher Performance: The Use of Variance Partitioning**

Analysis, VPA", published in *Education Policy Analysis Archives, Vol.13, No.30, May 6,2005; ISSN 1068-2341*; Arizona State University and University of South Florida. It is also included and published in the prestigious research on-line portal, Education Resources Information Center (ERIC). At present, the genius is nominated for the prestigious Yidan Prize for education research and development because of his innovative VPA Model. The Yidan Prize is roughly analogous to the Nobel Prize. It was founded by Dr. Charles Chen, a Chinese billionaire, to recognize outstanding scholars in the fields of education research and development.

While I consider myself a most fortunate former student of the illustrious mind, for being a recipient and beneficiary of his invaluable precious books, again, my limited neurons just apprehend one truth: a rare genius lives in the Philippines, and he continues to walk to the zenith, far more decent [of course, good God!] than the despotic brilliance of the Aryan anti-Christ, and a lot more human than the superfluous intellect of Einstein though they share the same first morpheme of the English alphabet in their first names: A for ALICIAS and A for Albert Einstein, A and A, but not necessarily direct correlates!

Darkness seemed to have hovered upon him while in the celebrated hallways of the country's academic pride and bulwark of many cries and voices, but this intellectual of true grit rose to his redeeming glory. Unlike King Ozymandias, he refused to become obsolete and remain fallen, but like the King, he had his moments of defeat from brazen betrayal, dejection, and abandonment, tossed in the heat of a desolate desert. But not for long! Laurels came one after the other, and indeed, they keep coming his way even now in semi-retirement.

"...his horn shall be exalted with honour" [Psalm 112:9}

For all his hard work, perseverance, and selflessness, God

has rewarded the man in very special ways. This list of local and international awards, plaques, and recognitions indubitably puts him on top, a cut above the rest:

1. **Guinness World Record Certificate;**
   Re, **Humor and Madness;** has a World Record Preface of 8632 Words, but has only 3251 words In the main body of the book

2. Listed in **Outstanding People of the 20th Century;**
   International Biographical Centre;
   Cambridge, England

3. Listed in **Who's Who in the World;**
   The Marquis Who's Who Publications Board, September Edition, 1999

4. **Distinguished Member, International Society of Poets (ILP)**

5. **Certificate of Merit for Distinguished Service,** which is the subject of notice in **Volume XXVIII, Dictionary of International Biography**

6. **Life Fellow, International Biographical Association**

7. **Outstanding Ilocano Educator (2005);**
   University of Northern Philippines; Vigan, Ilocos Sur

8. **Centennial Professional Achievement Award (2018)**, University of the Philippines, College of Education Alumni Association, Inc.

9. **Community Service Award**;
   Cainta Greenpark Village Zone 1, Cainta, Rizal

10. Member, Board of Directors, ***Gunglo Dagiti Mannurat nga Ilocano***, Ilocos Sur Chapter (GUMIL); meaning "Group of Ilocano Writers"

The exceptional intellectual's stellar teaching career at the University of the Philippines, Diliman, which spanned twenty-two years [1979-2001], saw him mentor hundreds of students who would emulate his passionate commitment, if not obsession for excellence and dynamic leadership, participation, and contribution in education, research, mathematics and statistics, the sciences and the arts, outreach and community service; not to forget, in humouring humor and the universe. Only this man of unusual intellect finds perfect humor in the poetry of asymptotic love by lovers straight and straight curve, in the excessive adultery of a dilated haiku and ingenious Philippine *bugtong* or riddle, and in the tragic fate of a fool, in the character of Pedro, who, after basking in paradise with his neighbor's wife, witnessed accidentally by the husband himself, sits to play mah-jong, unmindful of his crime, then stabbed to death by the "cuckolded" husband but again "he did not mind that he was already dead"—the moral of the story being, "do not play mah-jong after committing adultery" [Alicias, 1997, HUMOR AND MADNESS].

"Emely, *maawatam diay* VPA model ko?" He asks me via text message in one of our disjunct coffee breaks on a not so mundane February afternoon.

"Oh Sir, it really is astoundingly brilliant, but my apologies *po*, I understood nothing!" My words seemed to quibble on my *celfone* as I replied out of sheer disappointment for my few neurons! [And this justifies the discussion of the VPA model in the Appendices by Aurelio "Jun" Ramos Jr., a former UP-Diliman math/statistics professor, now school owner of BEREA, an innovative science and arts basic learning institution. Jun is also a PhD student, and is currently writing his dissertation on the practical application of the VPA model.]

The impressive academic achievement and education of this "unusual" Filipino, outstanding both in numbers and letters, include a Graduate Diploma in Economics of Education and Education in Developing Countries from the University of London, England, as a British Council Fellow, a PhD in Educational Administration from UP-Diliman, an M.A. in Education from Mariano Marcos State University, Laoag City, and his Bachelor of Science in Education, math major, *magna cum laude*, which he earned at Divine Word College, Vigan, Ilocos Sur. His genius is quite a given and evident, but his genius in letters, poetry, and the arts is more than perplexing. He is indeed one rare breed of a homo sapiens, born in CABULOAN, STA CATALINA, ILOCOS SUR, but grew up in SAN JULIAN SUR, in the capital city of VIGAN, now one of the TEN GREAT CITIES IN THE WORLD. It is not very much surprising then if he writes like Miguel Cervantes De Saavedra as CIUDAD FERNANDINA used to be ruled by Spanish Conquistadores, with their legacy of quixotry.

Wow! The protagonist, ERIMAKO, lover, tragic hero, or fool [Humor and Madness 1997 and Humor and Madness, Jr., 2009] has taken roots in a 1.6-hectare farm [ERIMAKO'S FARM], right at the heart of the old Ciudad Del Castillian! This is now the haven of the *sobre saliente* Ilocano intellectual, where he spends much of his leisure time when not writing magnum opuses. Ah, he is especially proud and sentimental of two rare pieces of arrantly passionate poesy of sculpture, which he himself designed out of his spectacular imagination--ERIMAKO AND SALVACION! Oh, Erimako evolves and transforms, transforms and evolves infinitely like the man's

Regression Analysis. He tells me, "Those two pieces of sculpture are the main features of my ERIMAKO'S FARM!"

SALVACION! SALVE! The quintessential embodiment of an unexpected dream, of Pygmalion and his Galatea; a goddess of beauty; in the ode, not to a Grecian urn, but to subliminal bliss, giving my gracefully aged professor some kind of, say, a beta coefficient of 0.193 happiness, and a significance level of $p = .001$ excitement.

Oh, but Salvacion, Salve, has always been the exceptional Ilocana pharmacist and chemistry GURU, "My teacher, My wife", even long before this mysterious dream came to life on a fine exquisite piece of three-dimensional art! This, I suspect, for love also takes on many faces as the years come and go, with the changes in climate and weather, the seasons of rain, sunlight, deluge, drought, and calm, and the occasions of birth, adventure, struggle, victory, serenity, ailment, and death. Yet, he is to verse this legend, this epic, this mystery, this reawakening, this excitement and stirring in his heart and soul, with the unerring aid of his perfect Regression Analysis.

"She is Ma'am Teresita, Sir! Believe me!" I tell him, with my black coffee, enjoying in a new mug of multi-coloured fine feather and geometric prints, given to me by Lhevy, my M.A. English Language Studies advisee, whose recent proposal defense more than excited my four neurons with my former dean obsessed with the instrument of the descriptive essay!

TERESITA RAQUEPO-ALICIAS, the brilliant chemistry professor [MS in Science Teaching, DSLU, and BS Pharmacy, UP-Diliman; retired UNP professor, and former faculty, College of Liberal Arts, Divine Word College, Vigan].

THE BELOVED WIFE. She has always been his real, one and only queen---in his heart, in his soul, in his home, Mother of his three children.

I could not hide my much greater admiration for my professor, of once upon a time, as I listened to him tell me the story of their love: EDUARDO AND TERESITA., Ed and Tess. My tears kept rolling and falling in silent memory of my own one and only love. But my tears were in my segmentals and supra segmentals as my teacher's love prosody unravelled its beautiful overwhelming rivet of passion and romance, fun and adventure, tears and sorrow, hope and faith. Oh, what a love story of brilliant minds, of a pretty chemistry professor and her young dashing college student! Six-year age difference doesn't really matter for star-crossed lovers, oh, math and science-crossed lovers! Indeed, age is no antecedent neither intervening variable, where love is all that counts!

"Then shall the earth yield her increase; and God, even our own God, shall bless us! [Psalm 67:6]

The power couple, Ed and Tess Alicias, have been blessed with three equally brilliant and talented offspring: 1. Lillian, the eldest, has an MS and BS in Chemistry from UP Diliman, and where she likewise taught Chemistry in its College of Science. She is happily married to Emmanuel S. Ramos, who holds a PhD in Chemistry from New Jersey University, and currently works as Department Manager of an American electronics company. The couple is blessed with one child, Mikaela or Mika, who is a graduating Senior High School student, and has recently qualified at Stanford University to pursue Aeronautics Engineering. She is set to attend the university's summer orientation. Mika excels both in academics and martial arts [taekwondo]. In 2017, she bagged the Gold in the Taekwondo Bantamweight Division, 4th National Women's Martial Arts Festival, and the Bronze in the recently concluded NCR Taekwondo Championship. The young lady is a member of the Philippine National Taekwondo Team, Cadet Division. She has likewise earned medals in Math and Science; 2. Irma, the second child, is a Doctor of Medicine from UP Manila, and currently, a radiologist in a number of Metro Manila Medical Centers, mainly at Medical

City, Pasic City. Previously, Irma also taught Chemistry in the College of Science in UP Diliman, like her older sister, Lillian, with a similar undergraduate degree, BS in Chemistry. She is blissfully married to Architect Leonardo P. Veroy. They have twin daughters, Leona and Ima, who are still in elementary grades, and just like their older cousin, Mika, the twins are academic medallists; 3. Eugene, the youngest and *unico hijo*, is a navigation engineer in Seabed Geosolutions, a multinational oil exploration company. He earned his BS in Electronics and Communications Engineering at the Technological University of the Philippines [TUP]. Eugene is wonderfully married to Wilfra or "Pinky" G. Gamilla, who works as a Project Assistant at the United Nations Development Programme. Pinky has a BS in Human Development Management from Assumption University. Eugene and Pinky have three children who are all achievers and medallists, also in the fields of Math and Science. Eunice and Elyssia are SEA-DEPED awardees in Math and Science as well as DOST-YES [Youth Excellence in Science] awardees. Elyssia is also an outstanding gymnast; she emerged the ALL AROUND CHAMPION in the recently concluded 2019 Philippine Cup. Her Team SPSCP came out Second Place Team Champion. In the 2018 Philippine Cup Competition, Elyssia garnered five medals, also in gymnastics. She has likewise competed in Singapore and Indonesia. Of course, their youngest sibling, their one and only brother, Eoghan, is another achiever in Math and Science, with all his medals in Grade School. One day he went home very sad, and when his Lolo inquired why the sadness in his face, Eoghan answered: "I got a low score in my quiz; I got 98." Wow! As what they say, "*Kung ano ang puno, siya rin ang bunga.*" What a wonderful family of achievers, of course, with Sir Ed and Ma'am Tess at the helm of it all! Quite superior genes and exemplary modelling, nature and nurture in perfect harmony!

"From the rising of the sun unto the going down of the same, the Lord's name is to be praised." [Psalm 113:3]

In 2006, Fr. Manny Flores, SJ, sent to me a seventy-five year old man of faith. I helped him produce his biography, and wrote with my tears as my beloved older sister, MANANG ERLEEN just passed away from the cruelty of cancer. But I worked and persevered with my little lowly pen to share with the world the life story of a good man, who dedicated himself in bringing the Word of God to Filipino and American families, an apostolate he did for many years with his late wife in the United States of America. One October morning of 2018, by accident or by destiny, I was once reunited, on line, via Facebook with my genius professor way back 1984, when I was young and twenty. I was and still grieving and mourning the tragic death of my husband LORENZO, in 2017, from glaring medical malpractice that up to this day, has remained unpunished. But, from the very moment I saw the familiar face, and yes, even more handsome in years, of that brilliant man who taught and inspired me to look more and beyond what seems to be trivial and insignificant, like eggplants and crystal balls, always with humor, together with hindsight, insight, and vision, I could no longer contain my little pen's excitement to tell and chronicle the story of an unusually ordinary man, yet no ordinary at all, whose life has been destined greatness. There is no mistaking it for indeed, his life is a

BLAZING LIGHT
...in the GRACE of ONE JOURNEY!
So, here thus begins his story;
The legend of a tale, the tale of a legend of the
WORLD'S SEXIEST MIND!
What pity if that life remained a secret!
What waste if that mind never humoured!

…how much more wretched my destiny,
Had my lowly pen not learned from my professor,

**THE HUMOR OF MISERY
AND THE MIRACLE OF LIGHT [EBO 2019]
ADDENDUM A PRIORI**
HERE UNFOLDS

THE STORY

OF THE WORLD'S
SEXIEST MIND

PART ONE
THE MEETING OF TWO GREAT BOOKS WITH ONE LITTLE BOOK

A. Prologue to the Sexy Mind

"Emely, what are you going to do with my life?" He laughs but is pleasantly surprised as he eats his pink salmon with his hands. An Ilocano. Like a true sage.

My son and I are seated two tables away from the side entrance. Max Restaurant has relocated at the new Annex Building of Sta. Lucia Malls in Cainta, Rizal. Oh, it was just like yesterday when we would frequent this place as one big family with Manang Erleen as the gracious hostess and organizer, which my Lorenz also enjoyed, as a welcome breather from all the stress in the academe. At past three o'clock on a lazy Saturday afternoon, it is surprising not to see a crowded favorite Pinoy restaurant, although I found it more convenient for tete-a-tete especially with the erudite. He is nowhere in sight yet. That's all right. After mother and son kept him waiting for almost two hours at the newly renovated Vigan Cathedral, December 31, 2018, several hours before the clock ticked 12 a.m., and ushered a new year! And we failed to catch him before he thought of walking back home to his kingly estate of 1.6 hectares, right there at the city of sentimentally romantic, and oh, colonial history.

"Mama, I want this a la carte. JP points at the menu. I order the same as the big plate has a moderately sized piece of crisp brown fried chicken breast or leg, tasteful creamy tofu, *tsinoy* pancit canton, single cup of plain immaculate white rice, maybe jasmin or *sinandomeng*, caramelized sweet potatoes [oh God, my signature subtleties!], plus meaty *siomai*, and gruelling to the bite- and- chew, yummy *butchi*, or a piece of .03 squared caramel brownies. Well, quite affordable for a widow of part-time teaching load in an average, regular Graduate School, research consultancy, and editing on weekdays and even on Sunday afternoons[!], but of course, evening mass at the CHURCH OF THE HOLY SACRIFICE in between short naps and those variables of x and y plus the extraneous, while creative writing, fiction but mostly non-fiction [memoirs, biography, and autobiography, with experimental novelty genres, still secret though between me and my paramour of print, my lowly pen!]], wailing, more wailing, then weeping, until the KISSING OF THE HOLY FEET OF THE MAN ON THE CROSS [ORILLOS, E.2019 in the works!], for most nights until daybreak, and oh, raising a dangerously handsome *unico hijo* who misses father-and-son nightly bonding with all those familiar and fascinatingly odd Philippine *bugtong* and *maikling kwento's*, not to mention tending to now ten colourful purring loud, medium, and low feline and one twelve year-old canine, our MARY NAZARENE PAULA ERLINDA CASOPEIA or Linda who licks my teary mid-life solitary face and fagged out feet, every now and then, all these on my frail but fighting shoulders every day, every night of my almost two years widowed life. How the cold sarcophagus had stolen in the freezing breeze my bliss of almost twenty-five years. I'd always thought as a little Indian war girl that all stones on earth were my allies! I was, of course, not aware THERE among the stones is life's greatest, most painful satire.

"I like *Sago at Gulaman*, Mama!" JP adds. So, widow orders two glasses of the sweet Pinoy drink, the cultural tongue. Oh, it's relaxing not to think much after an intensely colourful Master's oral defense. My four and only four neurons just could not understand how essay writing per se with the clear prompt cannot be the research instrument to produce the descriptive essay! Well, the pen and paper are of local necessity like food, clothing, air, shelter, and oh, gadgets [to the millennials like my son!]. Forgive me, dear God, I forgot my GMRC [sorry, SR. MARY CELINE SANTOS, SPC!], as I screamed, "You are out of order!" to my former Dean, who just won't let go of her almost thirty-minute interrogation or Gestapo on the instrument of Heaven knows, descriptive essay[!] of my tall, dark, beautiful advisee with a handsome bashful smiling-faced so fair, hubby, both from the mountains of breath-taking Antipolo. Well, the now Associate Dean, but admittedly very chic, sweet[oh!], and charming with mouth shut, has yet to finish writing her own PhD dissertation on how to read! Gee, thanks also to the eternal beauty of very motherly, DR. ANGELITA STA ANA, and the reserved intelligence of the smile-thrifty, DR. ERIC FABELLA, for keeping the sanity and decorum of academics with the sudden unlikely interlude of quack and more quacks during the intellectual exercise. Thanks also to the ever helpful, Mrs. Ellen Martinez for taking good care of me and JP in RCI.

Thank God, really, that has been an hour ago! I'm so glad to be out of the DARK AGES, both for my nine month-old computer literacy that has, oh, put me in the four century-old guillotine, now with me on leave from that famous university of the oldest dogma and repute, and the January afternoon's unleash of unbelievable intellectual conceit and or, arrogance, not sure if I were the victim or the culprit for the terrible crosses I've been carrying or dragging for all the long hours of fury and despair over the horrible inanities of medical malpractice. Thus, one of my FB posts begs for the curious reader to understand the psycholinguistics and psychiatry of my EPDM'S register. I sip my cold *sago* with relief and now, unexplained excitement. My lowly pen just cannot wait.

"Oh, there he is, Mama!" JP excitedly guides my eyes to a man on the move, in fact, with the graceful speed and evident acceleration of physics. But, do I also see Reverend Grayness blown gently by the fearful wind. I get nervous, and feel like wanting to pee before locking my eager eyes to those Emperor's Eyes!

He's wearing casual sporty clothes, and I think a pair of noble sandals or scholarly flip-flops, I'm not sure. I smile naughtily, but my heart gets the familiar surge of pain. My late husband, LORENZO QUIAMBAO ORILLOS, loved to wear his pair of blue BEACHWALK slippers even to his classes then in UP-DILIMAN on the last years of his teaching the country's top ISKOLARS NG BAYAN, before he retired in 2013. So, before entering RCI, his part-time job for twenty-seven years, he'd hide them in his Backpack, for the green entrance gate says, "NO SLIPPERS INSIDE!" Of course, his blue delight and footwear luxury made his classes perennially blackbusters, for the GREAT TEACHER was at his best, thanks to those flip-flops, best allies in old age and of eccentric scholars! I remember FR. FERRIOLS, SJ, who'd walk all over ATENEO DE MANILA on barefoot, intimating with damp earth, and kicking in disgust littered empty cans of capitalism and wanton consumerism, as I'd drive out of the carpark then my old red HYUNDAI [thanks to the Koreans!] sedan, after my POETRY and FICTION classes, shedding tears for EMILY DICKINSON'S "BUSTLE IN THE HOUSE," and cursing the violence and cruelty of dire poverty for MEXICAN ROFU'S "BECAUSE WE ARE SO POOR."

I try to forget my Lorenzo so I can brace myself for the approaching man in khaki walking shorts and regular collared shirt. I think he's wearing his nice beard too, but oh, Reverend Grayness is at least, an added attractive turn on, for this guy who carries an overload of everything there is to know, or maybe, we do not really have to know [skeptic me!] in this mortal existence. Oh, he's got Guinness World Record [GWR] in his Asian brown sexy hands! Well, I sort of expected he'd walk to our daytime rendezvous with libraries of the ages in his hands! But, of course, I silently wished before driving to the nice, quiet peaceful, and amiable mall, we'd talk of my little book, and my future book of one-month self-imposed writing deadline, instead of his books. Jesus! My four neurons are now agitated with the 98% probability that he'd force a sharp and formidable interdiscourse with me on his eternal fancy and obsession, Regression Analysis. I fork in nervous haste the delectable creamy *tofu* lest they'll be totally bland in the next seconds, and wash them with the now half full, half empty cold *sago*, likewise in frantic sips, fearful I'd choke with the apparition of the impregnable sage, cruising now my continents of current and real time of consciousness [Do I have an unconscious self? Well, let me ask him later!], and even my subconscious; and hence, I feel I just want to drift away, back to my desolate flotsam existence, rather than intimating my few neurons to his billions! But, oh, it's too late to retreat and run!

Oh, he's walking way too fast towards me! METEORIC COLLISION! Thank God, he stops midway like how my menopause halted my dreams for a more happily populated home! I move towards him with my son instead, and we shake hands as if we were just meeting for the very first time in the genesis of our memories. Oh, his hand is of the flesh, and of human blood; it feels warm and nice. The texture again

5

reminds me of my handsome Lorenzo who'd send me to sleep then by stroking my back, or massaging my exhausted almost dilapidated human anatomy as if it were a falling building of poor nails, and weak foundation due to graft and corruption. My God, he bends to offer me his cheek of THE WORLD'S WHO'S WHO!, but the Jew in SM North, tells me, I'm no VIP, so he's selling me the facial cream and lotion on a much discounted price with a free soap to unblemish my midlife widowed face! "What shall I do?" I ask my one and only one smarter neuron of four. Well, I give him as well my cheek of no-VIP, very shyly, as what my smarter neuron whispers, in the name of cordial felicity. Wow! Flesh to flesh! But, just mere brush it on, brush it quick for the flesh is weak! Gosh, what thoughts! I must be missing much my sexy hubby! He used to nurture his face with NIVEA CREAM, and how he smelled so good at night as he'd snore like a flirting buffalo! The Emperor's Eyes look into my preoccupied busy eyes of husband-memories, and oh, my heart beats wild, like the first time I sat in his class in 1984!

Today, 26 JANUARY 2019, I am reunited face to face with my very first professor at the UNIVERSITY OF THE PHILIPPINES, Diliman. Yes, after thirty-five years, I get to look again and pleasurably, [lustfully? hmmm] in those eyes of a REAL GENIUS, hear of Regression Analysis [as if I understood it!], and no sweat, break into the heartiest laughter, more laughter, and inevitably, guffaws [Never mind finesse, life is short!]. What really makes this date even more historic, at least for my lowly little pen? I'm going to ask this extraordinary man to entrust his whole life to me [Jesus!], in a matter of bites, sips, humor, humor *pa* more[!], sexy, sexier, sexiest word, words, long, longer, longest, ohhhs and ahhhs! When you are with Ed ALICIAS then it must be licking good, babe! Since my twelve year-old [though the law wants him in the calaboose when he stomps his brat foot!] is with me, and oh yes, all the time [!], I have already forewarned his cute tender mole*d* ears to automatically close, and focus on those computer games [not the viral *momo*!], once his mother's professor begins to lecture on all kinds of anatomies, sizes and shapes, even textures, colors, and scents! My growing son beams and grins at the prospects of acoustic linguistics.

This man of now ninety-seven per cent gray hair but still relatively fit in body and muscles [oh!], incomparably of an illustrious head [my God!], ere, intellect, who seems to look more of a saint [oh, not yet!] than the ferocious dangerously bold scientist, mathematician, educator, and many others [real polymath!] more than three decades ago, is DR. EDUARDO REZONABLE ALICIAS JR, one of the OUTSTANDING 20th CENTURY PEOPLE, one of the MARQUIS WHO'S WHO IN THE WORLD, a DISTINGUISHED MEMBER OF THE INTERNATIONAL POETS' SOCIETY, and the INTERNATIONAL BIOGRAPHICAL SOCIETY, the holder of a GUINNESS WORLD RECORD [re, Humor and Madness,1997]--not to forget all his internationally acclaimed books, articles, and of course, poems. Special mention of his own brilliant artistry and controversial yet delectable eccentricity is his poem, "ERIMAKO'S PEN" which actually earned him honorary membership in the elite and famous poets society. And, climactic [orgasmic, according to Prof. Jun Ramos!] of his contribution to world research and global education is his novel Variance Partitioning Analysis [VPA] model, praised and recognized to be more than pragmatically useful, and almost ingenuously brilliant as Einstein's Relativity Theory!

He puts his greatness on the now salmon*ed* and combo*ed* white rectangular but gracious table: a GWR, and he signs them in the swift unmistaken elegance of a life well-lived, and which continues to be as vigorous as the perpetually clandestined BANAOANG/ABRA RIVER. I hand him mine;

a little inspirational world seller [co-authored with FRANK T. VILLA], which I could not sign to give him as I only have one and only one copy, sent to me by a former PhD advisee, whose dissertation focused on the language of the country's sitting president, RODRIGO ROA DUTERTE. Well, bane or boon, he's now based in Florida, USA. Poor me, I cannot even afford Amazon.com to buy my own little biographical religious book ["75 YEARS OF JOURNEYING IN GOD'S GRACE", c2008, ISBN 978-1-4343-4667-4, AUTHORHOUSE U.S.].

I try to guess what he's thinking as he flips the lowly but delicate pages of the first book I've ever written. The genius smiles. His grayish beard is quiet. His sexy mind prefers it that way.

For as long as he does not take back my grade of 1.75 85%], I think that's more than good enough.

But now, here I write of that:

SEXIEST MIND!

PART TWO

BAKYA OR BAREFOOT, THE MAN FROM VIGAN WENT TO SCHOOL!

"Nothing special because of poverty!" Sir Ed says of his childhood. He continues, "I was bullied by a girl because I wore *bakya* [wooden wedge footwear] to school!"

The author of a world record [GWR] book surprises me and amuses my child as he narrates how his female classmate humiliated him for not wearing a decent pair of shoes or sandals to class. He was eleven years old and in Grade Five.

I cannot believe my ears as he shares the cruel details of the sad experience. My son, JP becomes more attentive, and this time, the naughty smile is gone in his face for my twelve year-old knows that it's bad to bully classmates, or anybody else.

"She bullied me because I was poor. My father, Eduardo Alicias Sr., was a farmer, and also, a carpenter; while my mother, Martina Rezonable was a vegetable vendor in the old public market, now VIGAN PUBLIC MARKET". Sir Ed's face becomes serious, and his eyes tell me and my child of the hard life his family had then...the sad life he had growing up, with all its toils and pains. A moment of silence falls, His usual gaiety and zest are replaced by twin morose[ness], and pensive[ness]. I try to hold my tears, for two other familiar stories, closest to my heart, of the same theme, texture, and affect. A tactful discreet sigh helps instead.

"My father would fix and tie my torn *bakya* with rubber band to keep the worn out *lalat* [cheap leather] in its place. But if it was too damaged, beyond repair, I'd go to school on barefoot. I walked about two kilometers for thirty minutes or so from our house, in San Julian Sur to Vigan Central School, a public school. I walked that stretch daily. I had no *baon* [packed lunch] or allowance. My parents could not afford to give me any pocket money. I studied at the Vigan Central School from 1952 to 1958." The world's sexiest mind with the sexiest humor [ERIMAKO'S PEN, HUMOR AND MADNESS, HUMOR AND MADNESS, JR.; EJACULATES FROM THE HEART] reminisces from the heart, and that boy from Vigan comes to life again, as if he were just beginning with all the hardships and the gruelling episodes of his existence in all those years, in all those times of tears, of a life devoid of comfort and bliss. JP is a cherub in respectful silence now, and glances at the great man across him and his mother with evident reservation, perhaps knowing the seriousness of the faithful tale, or maybe, out of his guilt for being a brat at times though his widowed mother tries to put on the decent table the agriculture and the fastfood of the universe in the midst of her wailings, weepings, and woes, well, including her sins of wrath and at times, therapeutic or vapid cursing.

Except that the lad had parents who did not give up, parents who quietly toiled, day after day, from sunrise to sunset, from the rainy season to dry months, from one misery to another until roses would just be for the grave, not for the living to enjoy and smell. But the tough ILOCANO spirit kept them going despite life's atrocity and tempest, in spite of the mean side of fate. Eduardo Alicias Sr. finished his education up to Third Year High School, while Martina Rezonable-Alicias stopped schooling by around Grade Four because of poverty. The couple knew their spirit was all they had to battle the cruelty of hand- to- mouth existence. Survival of the fittest.

Sir Ed's voice seems to crack as he continues deeper into his recollection of his ordeals as a child, of their family's sorry lot of existence. The sentiments of that child, of that boy are all over the World's Who's Who, the Outstanding People of the 20th Century. But, he soon recovers as he tells me and JP that he managed to graduate as the Batch Salutatorian in 1958. Nonetheless, the pensive mood resurfaces as he looks back to that time and phase of his life with all the details and the dark secrets. "Probably, I could have graduated Valedictorian had I not been the son of a farmer." The Emperor's Eyes seem to hold their tears. I am touched to the very core of my humanity that my soul wants to quash all forms of discrimination and oppression. Yes, if only I had literal wings to fly; I just lost even THE WIND BENEATH MY WINGS [my beloved!]. Worst, to a tragic death!

Listening further to Sir Ed, I can feel the resentment for blatant prejudice and appalling favoritism. Just like in any other nook and cranny of the world, regardless of historic epoch or age, the poor, the have nots are usually, almost always treated poorly, badly; while those who have in life, those who steal much and manage to escape the law, those who exploit the weak, the powerless, the impuissant, and those who hoard their excesses of wealth are, oftentimes if not always, treated so well as if they had two heads, two pairs of necks, and an extra pair for every pair of human organs, or one more for every single part of human anatomy. Oh, have they not been buying also the cells of sheep and lambs to keep their skin and face looking forever young? Poor biblical animals! Well, the science of excess is directly proportionate to the culture of affluence and or, excess; hence, too much leads to abscess, societal abscess. My thoughts can kill me as I now struggle with my lungs. The restaurant's temperature rises as my professor's reminiscence gets more stressors from a past that is deeply entrenched in the human soul and spirit. My one and only one smart neuron prefers to do empathetic listening now more than the critical to feel him, the great man of great science; oh, he seems hardened again by the burden of his past. His face is the look of repulsion, repugnance, resentment. I try to soften him with his soup of blushing salmon. "Sir Ed, you might want to continue with your salmon as it might get too cold." I gently move the bowl of the fresh sea nearer the sullen Emperor.

His eyes become more alert as he adds that the Valedictorian was a teacher's daughter [oh, maybe the nasty girl who bullied him so much for his *bakya*?], but I just murmur that in my head. That parent, that teacher taught in their school! Oh, the faces and forms of politics! But, we both sigh as we know these are truly terrible maladies in the country's educational system that are hard to beat, for they evolve, and quantum leap. However, the maroons in us make us resolve to write more books for the upkeep of minds as we then juncture with the welcome incidence of more collaboration in the future.

Then I ask him, with the sudden flight of a huge butterfly in my own memory of my childhood, "Sir Ed, did you ever have a puppy love? How old were you *po* when you had your first crush?" His eyes wander a bit in a second of time, but they begin to sparkle with the bubble of some titillating memory. JP's ears seem to be those of loquaciously cute elves.

"Ah, there was Angelita! I was in Grade Four. I liked her as she was a pretty girl. I had a rival, Arnold, who was then in Grade Three. I carried Angelita one day, so did Arnold; he also carried her! We hugged her tightly as we carried her!" The Distinguished Member of the International Poets's Society just cannot contain the boyhood romance, with all its sweet innocence and folly. He breaks into clean, nontoxic laughter. "Angelita did not cry, Sir?" I interrogate him like I were a social worker." Oh, she did! Angie cried!" The genius behind the cataclysmic impactful VPA model breaks into a resounding guffaw that maybe the historic BALANGIGA BELLS would not dare to challenge. The sexy mind with the sexy humor is back! JP covers his mouth as he laughs with the genius. My son is enjoying the new menu on the table: CRUSHES!

"In high school, I wrote six [oh, six indeed!] Love letters for a girl! By the way, Arnold, my rival then (elementary days) to Angelita's attention became a PALANCA AWARDEE." He smiles with the wit and mischief of a boy and an accomplished man. But, initially, he doesn't want to reveal the name of his high school crush." Maybe, she's one of those pretty, now silver-maned dignified women in their recent reunion photos!" Oh, finally, he said it's Jocelyn. I silently muse to myself, also tickled by the memory of my high school boy crush. But I had girl crushes too, dear God! I went to ST. PAUL, VIGAN for my secondary education, and that time, we were all but female species, who, maybe, delighted ourselves with our own class and gender. Ah, how youth can be so gullible but perfectly blissful for its candid, mirth, and adventure. JP tells me one day, as I was doing our budget on our bed of sentiments and prayers: Oh, Mama, I really will have to stay long in school. *Meron pang* BAR!" The innocence of my young son simply made my day, and my tearful heart cackled for the joyful gift of youth.

"I attended Ilocos Sur National High School from 1958 to 1962." Sir Ed now talks of his secondary education, also in a public school.

"Oh, Sir, I wasn't born yet when you were in high school! I was born in 1963!" I laugh naughtily as I unleash my indiscreet locutionary, but then I check myself in haste for I realize my illocutionary might not sit well with his perlocutionary. The genius might walk out of that glass entrance/exit door for his impatience and intolerance of my rogue stance before his elegant beard. But he chuckles with his discovery of my birthdate. He says, "Oh, you must be fifty-five, fifty-six now? You could have been my daughter!" I am quick to say, "Sir Ed, I'll be turning fifty-six come November of this year [2019] of our Lord!"

I don't know if my soon to be chronological age of 56 switched on the bulb of sensuality in his head as he suddenly leans a little towards me, with geometry in between us, and whispers: "Oh my father loved to read though he just got up to junior high. He had two books; a dictionary and an odd book in his cabinet! One day, he cut my hair; yes, he was a self-styled barber too. He sent me to get a shaver in his mysterious cabinet that usually he'd lock immediately after opening it. I soon discovered what was inside. That precious book of his was, 'Sexual Feelings in Married Men and Women' and, of course, I'd then secretly read it from time to time!" Sir Ed is very much his usual self; so green, plenty of green, more than green! "Oh, that explains it all!" I mumble to my four neurons.

"So, how about you, Sir? How old are you now, if you don't mind?" I remember that he's not a woman but a man [although the Benedictine monk, Fr. Vernard wrote an article on "Why Jesus Is a Woman", which I edited for SCIENTIA, the faculty journal then of SAN BEDA COLLEGE, MENDIOLA}, so, it's not rude to ask for his age, besides, am I not his biographer and memoirist? My voice is confident and clear, with JP perhaps guessing in his growing head, the age of the sage.

"I'm now seventy-three. I was born on August 10, 1945 [Oh, the Japs were gone from Philippine shores by this time!} I'm the eldest in a brood of five. My younger siblings are: Robert, Cleopatra, Florence, and Immanuel." Sir Ed gives his age in the language or register of science---precise, economical, factual [not that of medical malpractitioners!]. And he really sounds to me a responsible, supportive eldest child. But my heart is beating wild!

"Oh, my God, Sir Ed! You have the same birthday as my Lorenz! He was born on August 10, 1947! He was two years…a little younger!" My voice is both excited, and yet, pained.

"Really? Oh, I had no idea Lorenz had the same birthday! Yes, they said, they almost named me Lorenzo, after the Filipino saint, St. Lorenzo Ruiz!" My professor looks at me quite astonished, but with a certain tinge of hesitancy.

"Wow, Sir, what a coincidence!" I get the goosebumps now as JP stares wide-eyed. My segmentals and supra segmentals are more than marked now. And Sir Ed looks very different too. Maybe he feels a little threatened with the thought in his head. But, of course, how would I know what's exactly running in that handsome gray head, unless he shares them with me for our interdiscoursal dessert. But he keeps his silence again as the clock ticks before dusk. I see the black granite tomb with maroon edges in my now again heavy heart, but I try to console myself with the thought that my beloved is now feeding in heaven our feline that went before, together, and after his sudden demise in April of 2017. Besides, Mama Mary is watching over his grave, with her open loving arms, and her gentle beautiful praying holy face; our grotto is just beside the now resting place of my eternal one and only love.

Lorenz was Sir Ed's long-time colleague at the College of Education, in UP- Diliman. My husband was with the Department of Language Teaching, while Sir Ed was with the Department of Educational Administration. I look again into my professor's elegant eyes, and I see his fear of the riddle of coincidence. While time and space just maintain their own poetry of being, I fleet, flitter, and flutter in the highs and lows, the pains and joys, the glory and requiem of my own yesterday with my great one love. I never thought it would come to a tragic end, in the hands of students we mentored on our much younger years, the seasons of hope, dreams, and philanthropic commitment; in the hands of doctors we so trusted for their competence, integrity, and expertise; in the hospital we so loved to go to whenever we were of a sick body for more than two decades. "How old was Lorenz when he passed on?" Sir Ed enters into my whirling orbit, and I hesitantly whisper, 69, Sir. My professor of the sexiest mind and unbridled humor blinks, but he gives my late husband his respect. His tongue does not articulate his mind though the faint smile I see in his eyes gives me the hint of that rare quietude he so struggles to garb and dress his private thought, what with the two digits dangling in his sense and nonsense, an unexpected lull in the universe of the proverbial, of many possibilities. Maybe, this is an evolving Alicias Jr., E. paradigm on death and sex.

"I finished sixth of the graduating batch in 1962. I had to stop schooling for two years because my parents could no longer afford to send me to college. I worked then as a farmer/carpenter in those two years." The illustrious mind brings me back to my task as chronicler. He looks at me with sad eyes, but his voice does not crack, for he knows fully well, there's no shame working in the farm. But, of course, some morello in the countenance, as the time that was spent tilling the land in his youth could have been devoted to study and books. How destiny can be a much greater jester. My late husband also did the same so he could go to UP-Diliman, and pursue his dreams. And he loved books in as much as this genius before me voraciously reads and consumes the world of print. My four neurons, too; they love to fancy with the printed word and world with so many other worlds. The only problem, they just cannot absorb much as the two fine gentlemen, both my former professors in UP. I console, myself, however that I am ahead of them when I'm wearing my floral apron that comes in many hues. I can wash all the dishes in the world with little stories my lowly little pen wishes to tell eager eyes, and hopeful hearts, not so much with erudite minds [That's boring if you read with so much intelligence! trust me!].

"Oh, I hated Music because I was out of tune, I couldn't even hum the tunes of do-re-mi! I got 75%! I didn't have much interest either for Filipino as there was not much exposure to it. We had no radio, no TV!" Sir Ed laughs, his pragmatic philosophy grinning while the Max waiter begins to strut, and peep by our table, maybe wondering how much longer the odd but lovely company of a handsome gray head, cute growing head, and an aproned swirling head is keeping the purse for their obviously much tastier interdiscourse. I soon remember the title of one of the two books, Sir Ed just signed, with his "compliments" for me that afternoon: The Underlying Science, the Utility of Acquiring Early English Proficiency: The Flawed Mother Tongue Based Multilingual Education (MTBMLE) Policy.

"Well, Sir, that's understandable. I also didn't like much of Music for the same reason! But, oh, I loved Tagalog or Filipino as our relatives from Manila, Mamburaw, and Iloilo would usually come to visit, and they spoke much of this tongue!" I smile with the memory of my favorite maternal uncle, my late UNCLE ROLAND DEL CASTILLO TEJADA, who would come for short vacations from their house in Project 3, and teach us mathematics. Yet, my heart again sheds its tears for the sudden passing of my loving, so refined in ways and speech, Uncle Roland. He'd remind me every now and then to be more tactful, servile, and calm. He was truly one great lake of my childhood bliss.

"I went to DIVINE WORD COLLEGE, first as a Commerce or Accounting student. But soon, I shifted to Education (BSE, Major in Mathematics). I graduated in 1967." Sir Ed has a beautiful smile on his bearded lips as he now reminisces of his college education.

More city lights, the neon lights of cosmopolitan existence

are dancing now in my sight, literally and metaphorically, as my professor tells me: "I was in Second Year College when I met her. She was my chemistry professor." He beams with the delightful memory of his first one great love. I, too, beam with the unparalleled perfection of my happiness when I was nine and twenty. I also met my one great true love in the classroom of Applied Linguistics [EDL 205]. Yet, my heart weeps once more in silence.

"During weekends, my professor in Accounting would hire me for book keeping work. This was around 1964-1965. My professor in Spanish also did the same. Mr. Grappler (court interpreter) would then ask me to make translation work from Spanish to English and/or English to Spanish. This honed my English language skills. Around this time, Atty. Salacnib Baterina was my accounting classmate. Later, when he became an Assemblyman, he hired me as his Research Staff at the "Batasang Pambansa". I also tutored his eldest daughter, Celia." Sir Ed makes this recollection of his hard work, discipline, and training with the voice of a true achiever, a self-made man. He graduated *magna cum laude* in 1967. From there, he fiercely sought and pursued his graduate studies [Master of Arts in Education at Mariano Marcos State University, Laoag City,1976; PhD in Educational Administration, University of the Philippines, Diliman,1981; Graduate Diploma in Economics of Education and Education in Developing Countries at the University of London, 1985 - 1986, as a British Council Fellow.].

Indeed, the boy who went to school, either with his *bakya* or barefoot, the youth from Vigan who loved to compute from the cock's crows to the cricket's serenades, translating Senora to beautiful women; yes, he made it to school, brought home the medals to his loving, decent, and proud parents; while today, he is

A BLAZING LIGHT
In this planet, we all agree to call, EARTH.
THE BOY FROM VIGAN WENT TO SCHOOL!
"GIVE GLORY TO GOD"
ADDENDUM IN MEDIAS RES!

REMEMBER,
THIS IS
ONE SEXY JOURNEY!

PART THREE
CHEMISTRY, ROMANCE, AND ERUDITION

In the Eye of the Storm

"I recall that the term papers I submitted to Teresita were not papers on chemistry or geology but of my love and affection for her…"

Sir Ed sends me this text message a day before Valentine's Day. Wow! Tears start to fall on my face and roll down to the cold empty tiles of our modest condominium unit, JP and I call our "Rabbit's hole," with one room for our little zoo, the other for widow and child, but truly more than grateful to the kind-hearted military colonel who took us all in, this modern and new three-storey building he owns with his equally nice family; this wonderful grace of THE MAN ON THE CROSS for still grieving, mourning widow and her only child, now fatherless because of the cold mean scalpel.

I am more than touched by such rare expression of genuine affection by a man of great science, huge brilliance, so much depth. I cannot recall of a single instance during my UP days with this extraordinary professor when he would talk of his wife in such intimacy of his locutionary, and illocutionary, of his poetic, and metalingual, or of his phatic, and even ludic, especially of their romance, the getting- to- know- you - because I'm- in- love- with- you stage! The perlocutionary gets me shedding more tears as I feed each one of our now ten cats, each on its own fading-color-coded cage; of course, Kitty is always assigned the purple cage, while too frivolously playful Amanda usually purrs all night long in her pink or sometimes lavender. The rest, they take the blue, the gray, and the black; I wonder why my late husband and myself, including JP never looked for a yellow feline sanctuary, or maybe, we forefelt an unfortunate episode years later. I blow my nose with a toilet tissue, while Linda, our twelve-year old dog [JP's literal age!], so, now about ninety-six years of her current earthly existence [as I've always felt she must have been a great regal queen with the biggest heart ages ago!], stares at me lovingly yet oddly, maybe wondering why I'm already crying when it's not midnight yet, and I have not even kissed the HOLY FEET of THE MAN ON THE CROSS, hanging just beside her own nook in our so cramped lonely cosmopolitan abode. "Oh Linda, he's human! He loves her! He's indeed mortal, not the unfeeling, erratic Zeus of Olympus; and yes, refreshingly clear and resplendent, he's still very much in love with her!" I tell my patient, tolerant dog feverishly. The feeling is truly wonderful! The memory of "The Last Rose For Emely" somehow creeps in, making my heart cringe, twist, and cringe in a few seconds, stabbing my chest a thousand and dozen times, tossing me, fore and aft, the memories of such beautiful intoxicating blissful perfection of human love that was treacherously forestalled, cut, and ended by greed, greed, and greed! But, my Linda Cassopeia licks my unsteady feet, caressing...warming my shivering soul with the shining light that emanates from heavenly glory, and my forlorn turns into radiant hope; Sir Ed's undying love for his

FIRST AND ONLY TRUE LOVE! This realization of a former student on the humanity of her great intellectual former professor, now on top of the world, gives her another reason, another purpose to live her life despite its profoundly, fluently excruciating pain and misery: to write more biographies of real people who have lived real lives as living testimonies of God's greatest gift, LOVE! "Oh, Linda, my tears wish that I now write as they fall and roll…hush hush Cassopeia, no more need to worry and fret! Your star, your luster is mine to keep, print, and share. This is what He's whispering, Him whose crucifixion and death saved me and everyone from worldly and eternal death. Linda, just go to sleep now as your corner is dry, and my tears will soon also dry, as each tear shall make each word, each page, each part, each chapter…until a new little book is written and read. This is now my life's purpose, my new mission before I, too shall rest, with my beloved, beside the GROTTO OF OUR BLESSED LADY, under the mango trees of my childhood and adolescence." I kiss back my dog who smells sweetly of my pink shampoo with tovarich Tolstoy, both in my heart and in my thoughts.

In all those years, in all those toils and ordeals, in all those sins and pitfalls, until all the triumphs and victories, there is just but ONE WOMAN: TERESITA RAQUEPO-ALICIAS.

She's the UP pharmacy graduate, the excellent chemistry professor, the young Ilocana beauty and brains from SAN VICENTE, ILOCOS SUR [the town of sculptors like the old MATA who worked on our mother's life-size, and half busts!]. She, whom the young scholar and math genius fell in love with, in those delightful years of study and youth!

"In the classroom. I met her in the classroom. She was my chemistry professor in Second Year College at DIVINE WORD COLLEGE, VIGAN. Teresita is six years older." Sir Ed tells me, as he searches for the chicken thigh in his *arroz caldo*, at Max's Restaurant, the eternal rendezvous of professor and student of long ago. He speaks straight from the heart, without batting an eyelash. I bring my much eager ears much closer to the voice of a proud sentimental husband. I smile with the discovery that the couple met, fell in love, and taught at the DIVINE WORD COLLEGE of VIGAN [SVD-run learning institution]. The priests closest to my heart, JP's, my late husband's and our whole family are an Indonesian SVD PRIEST, FR. UBALDOUS DJONDA, and of course, FR. LEONARD SHANKAR ROSARIO, a BANGLADESHI REDEMPTORIST PRIEST, not to forget FR. ROY MATTHEW, FR. GEORGE, FR. MANNY FLORES, SJ; and FR. BIEN MIGUEL. Oh, I chuckle as the list of God's GOOD PRIESTS comes perching on my Max Combo Meal. How Jesus blesses me and my family with all of his good priests and nuns of course [SR. MARY CELINE SANTOS, SPC; SR. BLANCHE, SPC; SR. FIDELIS PORTILLO, SPC; SR. HENRIETTA; SR. VIOLETA; SR. TINE BAJARIN; SR. NILDA HECHANOVA, RA; SR. SARAH, SPC]. Sir Ed continues, "She was a beautiful and attractive young professor. I fell for her! So, I started writing her love letters; my term papers were actually compositions on my love for her!" My professor is definitely on memory lane while he spoons his *arroz caldo* in between his romantic reminiscence. I look into those emperor's eyes, and they twinkle with the memory though they seem to hold a little. I try to feel his temperature as he goes on to narrate the love story of two very young, talented Ilocanos whose paths crossed, not by mere coincidence but by the hand of destiny.

In 1968, church bells rang for the young brilliant couple. Their wedding was tagged as the top DWCV social event in that year by the school's organ (*The Immaculate*). Fr. Julio Barbieto, SVD, officiated the wedding at the ST. VINCENT FERROR PARISH in San Vicente. It was well attended by colleagues, family, and friends. "Typhoon FERIA destroyed much of our wedding photos!" Sir Ed tells me regretfully and emphatically as the horrors of that Philippine typhoon were truly catastrophic, having claimed so many lives, destroyed hard-earned properties, ruined too many dreams.

I remember how I cried and panicked as Lorenz was not able to come home during the night of another furious Typhoon ONDOY, a night of nature's fury and hell; JP was about three years old; his father was stranded in RCI, CAINTA, one of the worst hit areas of Metro Manila. "I'm just too glad to find one on the FB this wedding photo as published earlier on in *The Immaculate!*" Sir Ed speaks with a sigh as the beautiful priceless artifacts of delightful years are indeed more than real gems and diamonds. But, what can humanity do with nature's wrath, but to conserve and be responsible, prepare for the holocaust, and pray, not to forget, a handy bag of goodies, radio and batteries, plus a good flashlight, and oh, memoirs to give solace [75 YEARS OF JOURNEYING IN GOD'S GRACE, AND BLAZING LIGHT, IN THE GRACE OF ONE JOURNEY!].

As Sir Ed continues to talk of his wife, Ma'am Teresita, I begin to see sadness in his eyes. She got very sick, but after she has given him three wonderful, equally brilliant children. As a moment of silence falls between the *arroz caldo* bowl, that is now more than half empty, and the chicken combo meal, that is barely touched, Swinburne's "A MATCH" poem recites its first and fourth stanzas in my head:

> If love were what the rose is,
> And I were like the leaf,
> Our lives would grow together
> In sad or singing weather,
> Blown fields or flowered closes,
> Green pleasure or gray grief;
> If love were what the rose is,
> And I were like the leaf.

If you were thrall to sorrow
And I were page to joy,
We'd play for lives and seasons
With loving looks and treasons
And tears of night and morrow

And laughs of maid and boy;
If you were thrall to sorrow,
And I were page to joy.
["A MATCH" by ALGERNON
CHARLES SWINBURNE]

My eyes shed their tears in my heart, both for my professor and myself. Lorenz, my beloved husband now sleeps in eternal rest, while Ma'am Teresita can no longer function like her old usual self.

He had such an elegant queen, but the mean side of destiny just crept in to steal the joy and the glow of the couple. As Sir Ed tries to crack a joke in the midst of a painful reminiscence by his Dr. Ed, *de facto* M.D. too (doctor of medicine), antics and gimmickry, claiming medical know-how more than those greenhorns or even veteran medical sluggards, his eyes cannot hide how that serious affliction of Ma'am Teresita hurt him in all those years. I can feel his heart, hear its soft cries and regretful musings on wasted seasons of what should have been of their marital life; I can sense his temperature rising as he blinks with the threatening dusk. I now weep in the tragedy of two tales of love.

For the hours are long and empty
I bury the past for its ghost had been its glory
I scurry for the old gloves and the forgotten shovel
Yet, the earth is hard on my hand and heart,
I stare with the woman and the man who used to
kiss and laugh with the hours---

My steps lead me to where there is no rest.
I cannot bury the ghost for it is already but memory.
FOR THE HOURS ARE LONG AND EMPTY.

[---his widow, EBO 2019]

I SQUIRM.
YET, I CANNOT.
I HIDE.
BUT NOWHERE.
I BATTLE.
THERE IS NO AIR.
I FALTER.
---I AM SAVED. NOW, I CAN LIVE. BUT WHERE.

[E. ORILLOS 2019]

IF YOU WERE THRALL TO SORROW, Swinburne was a god who fell to mortality? How did he know it so well? Why did he know so much? HUMAN SORROW.

To Shakespeare, it's romance, it's a classic tragedy, Romeo and Juliet. Who doesn't know them? A cliché of love.

To Alicias, Jr., E., it's Regression Analysis. The **VPA** model, Humor and Madness [1997], and Humor and Madness Jr. [2009], Guinness record making, masterfully crafted books of an extraordinary genius! A novelty of love.

Flashback.

During his last year of college schooling in 1967, Sir ED was hired (despite his being a non-graduate then, evidence of shortage of math-science teachers) as a Math and Physics teacher at the Immaculate Conception Academy (Batac, Ilocos Norte) and Sta. Rosa Academy (San Nicolas, Ilocos Norte). Thereafter, in 1968, he began to teach in his Alma Mater, Divine Word College of Vigan. As a high school Science and Math teacher, Sir Ed inspired his classes with his dedication, creativity, wit, and humor. Even the most difficult and notorious of youth listened to the passionate lectures of the young, budding great thinker, and would-be man of revolutionary science. A year later (1969), his eldest child, Lillian, was born, who would then follow the footsteps of her brilliant parents by pursuing BS and MS degrees in chemistry, also at the University of the Philippines (Diliman), and where she would later on also teach chemistry to undergraduate students.

Typical of an Ilocano, Sir Ed knew he had to further his studies for much better opportunities in life, especially that his family was getting bigger--with Irma, the second child born in 1971, and again, just like the eldest Lillian, pursued BS Chemistry as well in the country's top state university. Yes, history loves to repeat itself in the Alicias's brood. Irma also taught chemistry in UP-Diliman, but later on studied medicine in UP-Manila. The youngest, and only son, Eugene, was sired like a test tube baby, for Sir Ed claims that he was inspired by a Reader's Digest article, following to the letter the medical procedure on when, how, and what to do so the Y (male sperm) would surely meet ovum, and *hola* [!], a sure baby boy! A young father with a very scientific mind, combined with mathematical prowess, he predicted a hundred per cent success of his experiment, with of course, his still then very up-and-about, smart, and lovely wife, Teresita. As he recalls of how his son, Eugene, was conceived via the tips of right timing during the ovulation of a woman as well as how deep one should make the penetration, Sir Ed is the perfect picture of high satisfaction for superior performance and superb experimentation. Eugene now rides a French-Norwegian oil exploration ship as Navigation Engineer. The proud father beams as he talks of his three very successful children.

Well, the young intellectual enrolled himself at the Master of Arts in Education Program of Mariano Marcos State University in Laoag City where he earned the degree in 1976. Around this time, he was already the Principal of the Immaculate Conception Minor Seminary in Vigan [from 1972-1977]. He tells me, in between spoonfuls of his remaining *arroz caldo*, that he mentored a lot of priests, including Bishop David William Antonio of Ilagan, Isabela. I learned that he was also the science and math teacher of several of our relatives in Santa. I am yet to tell him that my first cousin, Angel "Obong" Batin Martinez, was probably in his science/math class too, as our distant relative, the late Arthur Sabalburo was a classmate of Obong, one of my favorite first cousins I'd force out of the full Cubao-Quiapo jeepney to accompany me [on the first two weeks of freshman year!] to the Royal Pontifical University, located in the easily flooded Espana, Manila, later on during our college days. Obong is now working at the U.S. Postal Service, and married to my old high school classmate, Rely, now a dentist. Funny though how our other Paulinian classmate, Wendy Reyes, would climb our mango tree by the garage just to be able to take a peek on my seminarian cousin who, then looked very saintly, but whom our AUNTIE MAURA would usually keep inside their large concrete-and-wood conservative house. During those times, wood was the in-thing in housing architecture and fine arts in our hometown. I remember that we'd usually visit Obong then at the Minor Seminary, not knowing that their Principal would later on become my first ever professor at the University of the Philippines, Diliman, come 1984."

"How was it like teaching in a seminary, Sir Ed, especially that you were their principal?" I would later text him, on another wide-awake Thursday noon, after our second face-to-face interdiscourse at Max's with JP.

The genius narrates in his email: "In the Seminary, a few naughty seminarians punctured once or two times the tire of my bicycle, rendering me in a moment of distress. Yes, I used to bike to and fro the Seminary. I cannot forget how the father of one graduating seminarian who lost being the valedictorian threatened, pressured me [with gun visibly tucked in his waistline] to change and increase the grade I had given his son. The father was a government bureaucrat closely allied to the then reigning political dynasty of Ilocos Sur. Despite the grave peril to my person, I stood pat on my ground [the grade I had objectively and fairly given to his son]. The following year, I was promoted to the principalship."

"Wow! The mark of a principled, self-made man! From a nobody to master, from nothing to everything, from destitution to success!

I remember my own father, TEOFILO "ELOY" SABALBURO BATIN, and my late husband, LORENZO "LORENZ" QUIAMBAO ORILLOS, who were once a fisherman, and farmer respectively, took on bravely life's ordeals and hardships, struggled with their sweat, blood, and dreams until they reached the top of their careers. Such fine, rare men these three: my genius prof, my disciplinarian father, and my loving late husband. When men are this breed, who would care to be a spinster? Let their tribes increase! By all means, procreate the good seed of ADAM. Did not God, the Father command, "GO FORTH AND MULTIPLY"?

"Anything more special of the seminarians, Sir Ed?" I tease him with my now last peso Smart load that lunch time, with my tummy unsure of whether to have rice or just the *sinigang na baboy*, with plenty of tomatoes and no *utong* or stringbeans to veggie the pork in cubes.

Now, the green mind, verdant as ever, replies: "Well, boys are boys, wherever they were/are. The seminarians [teenagers] took any and all opportunities to take a peep or peek [intended or otherwise] at the thighs, boobs, etc. of their female teachers!"

Thank God! I totally ran out of *celfone* load at this point! But, a shocking episode of my short teaching stint in a Major Seminary at the outskirts of Metro Manila flashed suddenly in my mind. Oh, my seminarian student in World Literature who'd usually ask permission to leave the class, I'd catch in a romantic act with the young beautiful mother of his best friend, while some three other seminarians were inside the cubicles in that rather big restroom, with a common large mirror [powder room] area before the female and male CR'S. It took me more than a week to report to the new Dean [U.S. schooled!] the unexpected incident which I witnessed before the clock ticked twelve noon for the Angelus in the Seminary. I was torn between extending compassion to the unlikely lovers and my responsibility as an educator [and, what is it, really?]. The Rector, a very humble, congenial, kind-hearted young sacred person in his early forty's then but who was sickly, came to UP-Diliman, right there at the old large office of my husband, which had all the books of the galaxy[!], together with his architect-priest best ally. Oh, it was like talking with the angels and saints in heaven! Unfortunately, the new Dean decided to keep the erring seminarian for one more semester, hence, the Seminary could just offer the teaching load to my saintly husband, Lorenzo, as he was already teaching with them for three years before they thought of giving me the fiction and non-fiction of the continents through the ages, one Holy Week, a Maundy Thursday, as we went to the Seminary for *Visita Iglesia*. In other words, the holy men no longer invited me back to teach the Seminarians of the literatures of the world, the orthodox and unorthodox thoughts, the satires and the comedies, the saint in men and the doomed or the damned, the angelic and the fallen. I was therefore an outcast of the holy orbit for reporting what my pair of astonished eyes saw five minutes before the Seminary knelt on the pews to pray, and thereafter, the bounty of the earth, to be chewed, swallowed, and digested. There was not a morsel for my being truthful. I felt the "DIVINE INFERNO" was all over me. My epiphany was to pluck my eyes like KING OEDIPUS, for our family's budget was cut short of seven thousand pesos, like missing

THE SEVEN LAST WORDS on GOOD FRIDAY! But my Lorenzo politely declined as he told the good priests [of course, I still loved and love them, forgave them too for their own human frailty as the Seminarian's uncle was a politician and business tycoon who'd donate his excess wealth to the Seminary!], he needed to be with his woman/wife as he was a man/husband, and with their little son, the still very playful and mischievous, JOSEPH MARY PETER PAUL LAMB [LORENZO ANSELMO MARY THE BLESSED] or JP, who'd run and run all over the earthly holiness of the Seminary.

Resting, the very nice and respectful driver [oh, sounds interestingly familiar with the classy scarf!] of the Seminary who was then applying as a PO1 could only shake his head like a handsome wise man, and resort to the Pinoy onomatopoeic "tsk tsk tsk!" as he safely drove us back to our old up and down modest green apartment with a greener gate along Xavierville Avenue, owned by a very kind, very gracious, beautiful "NANAY" who'd come give us bowls and plates of her fine cooking on barefoot as the cemented common garage was usually wet, with our neighbors from Paete, Laguna, washing everything of the earth's dirty linens with their mini washing machine and their diligent beautiful working hands. Except when they didn't annoy me with their rambunctiousness, while I'd remove the lice on Linda's head. Oh, Sir Ed must be wondering now why I've not made any bombastic reply to the verdant brouhaha of his more focused, more selective memory of those hormonal Seminarians. If only he were several ears away from me, then, he could eavesdrop into the scandal of my memory. And, how he would shake the universe with his thunderous guffaws. On hindsight, I am more than glad I discovered by chance or by fate the humanity of a holy earthly place. As what my dear old diocesan priest friend told me: "You're still fortunate, you didn't witness two Seminarians or even priests themselves torridly kissing each other!" And the cute recollection of me, and my two old girl pals [We were college professors then with one, a lawyer!} snatching the most good looking RECTOR of the MARYHILL SCHOOL OF THEOLOGY one full moon, dumping him nicely on Inday's ISUZU, with the stunned but overly delighted priest on his slippers, for the four of us to see the then controversial movie, "THE PRIEST" in Greenhills. Oh, those who sat near us made moans and curses over the frailty of the holy protagonist, and I was too uncomfortable for the RECTOR of such a respected School of Theology that even the "Iron Lady of the Philippines" went to sit in his classes for the salvation of her fiery sharp tongue. May she rest in peace! After the movie, I believe the good handsome priest resolved never to kiss a man except THE MAN ON THE CROSS. We took him home before the cock crowed three times.

Oh, if boys will always be boys, and men are men, will they always be men? I'm no feminist, at least as far as I know, neither a sexist [Well, I was once a young sexy English teacher except that my chest has never been a real bumper!], as there are more moments that I just see humans, yes, so many humans, including myself, but not upon the onslaught of a dreadful memory for its incomparable pain, too tragic, a lot more than Shakespeare's eloquence of pain, betrayal, and sorrow; oh, so much more elegantly ironic than Hemingway's suicide despite the greatness of his soul in print. How I persevered to finish reading his "OLD MAN AND THE SEA" as I chewed young fresh green *SARGUELAS* (Spanish plum) on my favorite tree. Was it then a pre-sentiment of my current life of chronicling the lives of exquisite septuagenarians? As Sir Ed takes our second planned yet truly impassioned interdiscourse to uphill and downhill climbs, to winding then tortuous roads, to left turns, right turns, and U-turns, even counterflows [!], to alleys and avenues, until the expressways, open fields, sweet valleys, and wonderful prairies, I can only laugh, blush, moan, and sigh for reality, no matter how ridiculous, ludicrous, or luciferous is true, truthful, and faithful to its nature. That's why the cliché, life is stranger than fiction, and Oscar Wilde's, "Life copies from fiction"; for reality, I believe is both coherent and incongruous, consistent and erratic, pleasant and horrible, crazy or more than perfect, sinful or much too sinful then less or least. Whichever, whatever, whenever, wherever, wherefore, therefore…

The Holy Bible says, "Only those with a pure of heart can enter the kingdom of God." As I listened one day to the Christian Pastor over DZAS [Thanks James and your nice Chinese mom for gifting me this radio!], I could not help but wonder how heaven must be so minimally populated, purgatory quite dense, and hell, unbearably overpopulated [Virgilian faith or filth?]. But worst, I worried for Sir Ed as his exploits and adventures, to my marginal moral compass have not been, in a way, venial! Well, I also have my sins. And as I now chronicle my genius professor's lustful, lusty, lustier, lustiest exploits and profusely carnal exorbitantly scandalous adventures, the faucet in our rabbit's hole cum menagerie [Thanks Sir Ed and Shelley!] makes its swift and long spirit, then erratic spews and spurts. I make the sign of the cross as now I cruise the waters to the world of flesh, more flesh, too much flesh!

Misery loves company, they say. To Alicias Jr., E., it is passion, more passion, orgasm, repeated orgasm. MORTAL SIN? But his existentialist self calls it, survival of the pragmatic being, and this being, can be a student, a scholar, a spinster, a widow, a commoner, a married woman, or anybody else with hunger for the flesh, sexual appetite. Oh!

In 1985, Dean Paz Ramos of the UP-Diliman, College of Education recommended Sir Ed for post graduate studies in London. He then vied for the competitive British Council Fellowship, with about seven hundred applicants. Only five were taken in as Fellows in different disciplines. Sir Ed, who was this time, a middle-aged man, boarded the plane to the world's land of great kings and queens, princes and princesses, dukes and duchesses, legends and fairytales, satires and tragedies, love, passion, and romance, including HARRY POTTER[!], to earn a graduate diploma in Economics of Education and Education in Developing Countries at the University of London. The other equally fortunate and brilliant British Council Fellows included: Napoleon Imperial (Commission on Higher Education, CHED), Atty. Carlos Medina Jr. (Ateneo), Benjamin Tolosa Jr. (Ateneo), and Atty. Danilo Concepcion, now the sitting President of the University of the Philippines.

For ten months or so, the middle-aged genius basked and wallowed in the wild revelry of passion and romance, sex, more sex, pleasure and much pleasure, studies and affairs, erudition and erotism, betrayal and infidelity, sin, lots of sin, and so much sin--while pursuing more light in the city of eternal dusk as the sun rarely shines in the skies of London. My father, Teofilo "Eloy" Batin would always speak of how the clouds hide the sun in that city as I and my siblings were growing up, for he likewise went to Cambridge University for his specialization in agronomy under a British-Australian Colombo Plan Scholarship Grant.

Worn out it may be, but the statement still is a startling statement, full of its own startle: Life begins at 40!

Eduardo R. Alicias Jr. meets one of Tokyo, Japan, in one of those London freezing mornings, on just another ordinary, lonely sidewalk for international students like him and like her. A passionate "sex weeks" [six weeks] would later on ensue from the casual but nervous, "Hi! Good Morning!", "Are you oriental?", "Me too!", "Can I visit you?", "I am Ed, and you are...?"

Keiko or KeeKee!

The forty-two year old Japanese woman, kept staring at

the approaching Filipino intellectual, smiled so sweetly and generously at him, with the exquisite enticing beauty of cherry blossoms, gave her delicate supple hand to the fellow Asian, and agreed to be visited at the co-ed John Adams Hall (Dormitory); one wing for the female, another wing for the male. Soon, the Filipino male was often, if not always, walking down the all-female hallway to the Japanese woman's Room; his was Room 321, and the math in his head sums up the three digits as Six or SEX, compatible a hundred per cent to the SEX or SIX of Keiko or KeeKee. His six got hooked with her six equals SEX, and more SEX!

Oh, the two University of London graduate students from the Orient seas became Adam and Eve, eating hungrily, rambunctiously, vociferously the forbidden fruit. They toured Europe in naked pleasure, forgetting all the honour for an adventure in sight, smell, auditory, touch, and infinite taste of flesh and more flesh until the male erudite peaked and exploded from the sexual exploit to a world record breaking ejaculation of his pen, but which he managed to preserve for about a decade [like Monica's controversial dress allegedly with Bill's sperm!] of wait-and-see to the Guinness World Record. The nom de plume, "ERIMAKO" was conceived, and borne out of that passionate tryst with the irresistible, incontrollable, and insatiable beautiful Japanese woman.

"Emely, heaven on earth is having an American house, Chinese food, and a Japanese woman!" Maestro ERIMAKO inserts himself into my private thoughts, and he laughs as I blush, though my ego and super ego strike an unexpected blow on the emperor: "Sir, did you feel guilty?" He fell into a moment of silence, then looked at me straight in the eye: "Yes, there was guilt, at the beginning. Then I just got used to it." The unexpected confession of my professor struck me deeper into my core that I wanted to pee in shame for my own sins, and in awe for the resurrection of the dead to everlasting life.

But, well, he's yet to be canonized, after this mortal life, of course!

"Only those with a pure of heart can enter the kingdom of God." The biblical verse kept hovering throughout the narrations of a genius on his follies, mistakes, excesses, faults, and sins as he desired for greater knowledge in the nectar of forbidden love, throwing himself in the quagmire of pleasure and wanton self-abandonment, just to give in to the sensual appetites, the erotic, base tendencies of mammals in the animal kingdom. Despite all the billions of neurons in his head, the man gave in and gave way to his libidinal, lascivious desires and appetites, as the millennial idiom, "lust *pa* more!"

"I often travelled to Japan in the next two years, always on KeeKee's expenses." Maestro ERIMAKO tells me, matter of fact. He adds that his eldest daughter, Lillian, was then beginning to suspect of his Tokyo sojourns, but which the maestro's mother would just dismiss as scholarly travels. His wife, Teresita, had been very sick even before he got the British Council Fellowship, which really was a tough situation he needed to overcome, for the sake of their three growing children, who were then all of school age. It was also around this time that UP-Manila offered him Associate Professorship, but which he also had to sacrifice for what he thought as a greater opportunity.

While Maestro ERIMAKO undresses euphemism for a totally no-holds barred interdiscourse with me, I felt the temperature was getting higher and more disturbing to my psyche, and well, sexuality, of course, because I am human too, as the Maestro later tells me via a hot morning's text message: "Huhuhu...*nagselfie ka* while reading my long one sentence? [referring to his Humor and Madness, Jr.]...eh...go ahead, you are also human!" I replied, "Hahaha! *si sir talaga*! Just in my mind, and I apologize for the telekinetic pornography as my reader-response to your one-long world record making!

Baka bumangon na po ang aking asawa mula sa kanyang puntod para ako'y kanyang batukan sa aking mga pinagsasabi! But well, I enjoyed your lust!" He goes, "Thank you for doing justice to my Humor and Madness, Jr."

As I washed the dishes with my soiled floral apron that morning, I whispered my penance within the hearing distance of my pets, of my ten cats, all in their cages, quiet and unmindful of the widow, and her little sins of delight in the face of too much adversity, for the murder of her husband, leave of absence by force of circumstance from the university she served so well, selflessly, in all dedication and humble expertise for thirteen years, billowing bills, depleted resources to nothing, while keeping a cool, nice, sane head for her growing son, studying in a middle class international school, with his classmates telling him, "Oh Joseph, you must be filthy rich as your Mama writes books we see in Google, and she teaches old people with good jobs! I laugh with my falling tears as I hug my dog, Mary Nazarene Paula Erlinda Cassopeia, or simply, Linda, given to us by two equally eccentric but brilliant and loving SPC nuns: Sr. Mary Celine Santos, SPC; and Sr. Fidelis Portillo, SPC. SR. Celine, the School President would then feed the convent dogs with the Sisters' bowls while Sr. Fidelis, the College Dean, would go around the school with her dog and her favorite junk food in one hand. They loved my husband Lorenzo more than me, I guess, for he was already a saint before he climbed to heaven. Of course, the SPC nuns adore our child. Linda licks my wet hands still with the soap bubbles.

Is human bliss just in a bubble? I remember the mouth-watering pink cotton candies just outside the ageless St. Catherine Church in Santa, situated half a kilometre from the old China Sea every Holy Week when our fully brown-veiled granny, Alejandra or *Lilang* Andang would take to the church three little girls, the younger ones out of a brood of six then [Eloida, Elrey, Erleen, Emely, Ely, and Estela Marie}, with five girls and one boy. How I envied other kids who held those yummy pink to their licking tongues that, in a moment, would be like bleeding flames, When our grandmother had extra cents in her purse, she'd let us buy them, with our bright ruffled little dresses dancing in delight, and our shiny black shoes with ribboned white socks jumping in excitement to hold, lick and lick those sweet pink! Oh, I'd waste no time to consume the heavenly joy lest I'd not enjoy it for I was too scared it might just melt, and well, it was already shameful for an eight year-old to lick it on the wooden pew, with the foot-and-knee prints, even sole prints of praying and prayerful humanity, whether they meant them or just simply reciting the words in their sleepy or porn heads or sinful lips. Oh, did I have those thoughts then?

"She had a portable typewriter, and I offered to be her typist for the essays she wrote in her English class." Sir Ed again breaks into my thoughts as I try to process every bit of sexual confession he has been bombarding me for about two hours of intense interdiscourse, unmindful of the TEN COMMANDMENTS, and the morality of the pious, the fanatic, the fondled, or fanged. Oh, thank you, Jesus, for the other table not upturned for my little bachelor whose ears are spared from the excessive vermillion of MAESTRO ERIMAKO'S Red District.

I struggle to switch roles as the sinner of the hour confesses. But, I get so confused if I should do more of expository listening, active listening, passive listening, critical listening, or empathetic-sympathetic listening. Oh, forget about objective listening as my blood pressure goes up and down, then climbs and climbs, I start to gasp for air! Ah, the waiter brings me in time another cold glass of water. Thank God! This confessing man is driving me crazy and thirsty!

"While I typed and edited her essays, KeeKee was busy with all the muscles of my body! Oh, she was good!" The septuagenarian with still a very green mind continues as he sips into his cold mango juice, giving Sheira, the Persian-looking waitress, flirtatious glances as she struts around our table like a peacock.

"Oh, how could you focus on the grammatical glitches then, and sure, you kept pressing the wrong keys, with KeeKee's magnum opus on your muscles, Sir!" I swing back the naughty blade on him, while I try to fork harder the juicy creamy *tofu*.

"Ah, that was no problem at all! Fixing her English was as mechanical as typing on her portable, since her sentences were so predictable and quite static! So psychomotor, so kinesthetic, no sweat! I just kept everything steady except at the point of orgasm. How could you be rigid at the peak of pleasure!" MAESTRO ERIMAKO turns into a roaring lion. His eyes though probe into my thoughts, and he tries to feel my core.

"Oh, quite empirical data, very good for error analysis!" I retort wryly. This time, my four neurons are hitting each other on my head. One asks, "Is this guy a pervert?" The other says, "Oh, he must have gotten too tired at the University of London, analysing those Third World economies, and how their educational systems can save them!" The third one hushes the two: "Hsssh, just enjoy his pornography! How often does an intellectual, a genius for that matter, confess his libidinous exploits? Besides, who has not masturbated, literally or the other, not even once in their lifetimes? Don't you recall your close friend, Mina, an ex nun? Didn't she confess how she'd get down to her knees to battle her sexual urges while she was in the convent, that she would writhe, twist, and cross her legs so as not to sin? But she admitted having masturbated several times even with her veil! She said she desired the convent's overly masculine driver [Oh, driver, sweet lover!]; but, of course, she was too shy to ask him give her a taste of Sodom and Gomorrha! Remember your bright student [top of the class!], Karen, who'd confess of her sexual repressions that she'd have sex with her old professor in her mind over and over again, though he'd pass on? Karen confessed she was a sex maniac in mind! And what did she discover one unassuming dusk? "Oh, Ma'am, I won't go back to that convent again! I just witnessed, past Angelus, Sister Itchy and Brother Horsey necking and petting by the swing in that garden of sacred words, steps, and images! Oh, how she moaned like a sex nympho! And how he ejaculated like a despot! Those reverend sex maniacs!" Karen was just overly disappointed of course. And, don't you remember those eaglets, how they interpreted Blake's "The Sick Rose"? Didn't all of them agree the rose was sick because she was always masturbating for the fool husband was more busy with his business, books, and golf? So that her petals were dry and shrivelled up? And also that same summer poetry and fiction class in Loyola, how did they understand Dumdum's "Mayon Volcano"? Didn't they also say, the eager tourists ogled the perfect shape like a naked man to a naked woman, with the best milk? And those boys in Mendiola years back, what have they been kissing and tellIing? How they would hire a high class pretty college prostitute, then line up, patiently wait for their turn? And how five male teachers would orgy with a cheap prostitute? How about that female theology professor who'd watch "TURO" live with her all-male class? etc. etc. etc. Wow! This third neuron of mine stored so many things! But on further analysis, it did not fake the other side of humanity, so good job! The fourth of my four neurons whispered to the three: He, Sir Ed, is to be canonized! Jesus, how my little brain managed to search for the thesis, anti-thesis, synthesis, and call to action on MAESTRO ERIMAKO'S discourses and confessions on human lasciviousness, sexual appetites, promiscuity, ennui, deprivation, angst, alienation, dejection, sexual freedom, culture, literacy, economics, travel, poetry, foreplay, flirtation, attraction, passion, loneliness, orgasm, scholarship, pretensions, dreams, fantasies, dishonour, sin, lust, guilt, and love. My fourth neuron seems to be correct! He's on his way!

Though the genius continued tempting and seducing my new-found moral compass and sexual management cum sex economics of a widow for almost two years, with his vivid, detailed, concrete sex narratives especially while in Japan---then, three times a year with a woman visiting him in his brothel, oh, motel twice a day [for a week], making love with him in the morning, then again, in the early afternoon, while the cherry blossoms just kept on blushing as they served mute but lovely witnesses to scintillating Oriental romance and overflowing passion, stolen from the Grecian watch of Hera!, my fourth neuron just kept me afloat, though almost giving in to the pleasure of lustful listening [Oh, did I ever lecture on this listening type to both my graduate and undergraduate English classes?]. Sin is quite a tempting sumptuous meal, especially when it's a Guinness World Record author who tells his tales of passion and lust! But, the Holy Bible and its verses just kept me balancing my canoe no matter how it careened left and right, front and back, as MAESTRO ERIMAKO continued to take me into his sexual exploits, the waters of his sin.

"Ah, again, in London, we really were drunk with the potion of passion and love so that while I typed and edited her English essays, Kee Kee would get me into the language of wanton ecstasy! How we'd desire each other, making love for hours worth all the golden moments of eternity. We were like the Trojan, Paris, and the Spartan Queen, Helen, so passionately fallen for each other! Oh, indeed Homerian pages of classic revelry! Our sex weeks in Europe were really most exhilarating, liberating, so fascinatingly salubrious to the corporeal entity of our beings!" And it was not just all sex but international economics and fiscal management too, oh the pragmatics[!], as my technical help was likewise sought by our African friends. Kee kee's portable was indeed at its optimum use. MAESTRO ERIMAKO is totally all fences down. He's absolutely fully naked before me now, so I drink another cold glass of water. "Oh, Sir, friends with benefits!" I gasp for more air.

"But, on August 10, 1988, my birthday, I received a letter from her breaking up with me. She wrote, "Let's end this!" Sir Ed's face gives away an old sentiment. His voice is low, almost hesitant with the words.

"How did you feel, Sir?" I ask carefully. I look into the emperor's eyes that the Japanese beauty fell in love with.

"Oh, it was painful!" Sir Ed is becoming more human. The recollection of this episode in his life brings the elegy of forbidden love. But, I feel better as I realize he did love her in a way; the woman was not just for his lust; the woman was also temporary partner, a human comfort. At least, not just for sex!

"Did you try to win her back, Sir Ed?" I'm more at ease now. The waiter brings some more water. My new glass remains, full but not for long.

"Oh, I tried but she cut off all communication lines, so what can I do? Anyway, I also courted the secretary of our Department at the University of London! And she seemed disposed to accepting my amorous propositions--except that, as events would later on show, her boyfriend is one of my two male professors! I had three professors there, one was female; all renowned authors! Of course, I backed off, or I'd get a failing grade if he would found out I was making out with his girlfriend, though he was also married like me!" Sir Ed laughs at the chance discovery of his respectable professor's affair with the voluptuous secretary.

"I also courted my classmate, a beautiful Irish girl. But then again, I found out from her that she was having an affair with my other married male professor!" At this point, MAESTRO ERIMAKO and myself could not control ourselves from laughing, making JP stop momentarily from his computer games, wondering what's so delightful in the menu! Thank God, Sir Ed had no sex story to tell of his female professor! Maybe, she was not really a human being, maybe a god-mother fairy queen, or from Shakespeare's "Midsummer's Night Dream!"

"Sir, did she know of these things you were doing?" I remember they were sleeping together the rest of their University of London days, and occasionally during the next three years.

"No, she did not, primarily because my extra moves had been thwarted from the beginning by force of circumstances! But she was also being courted by a British officer at the British Council Office, and one African classmate as well! Many were attracted to her too.

Sir Ed tells me matter of fact. I hear more of the pragmatic philosophy than romance and its jealousy at this point. Maybe, it was really hard those days to study in London! Everybody seemed wanting to go to bed with everyone! Why didn't Maslow include sex as basic necessity in his hierarchy of needs? I muse to myself, but levity aside, reality glares too overbearingly. Oh, my father went to Cambridge too! It was a 9-month specialization training he had. Well, I'm still scared with the leather belt, so I won't ask.

I thought my professor's sexual exploits ended with London, but I was mistaken as my ears were unprepared for more, in the next tales and confessions, right here in the Philippines! More affairs of my genius professor took place here in Metro Manila and all over Luzon, the Visayas and Mindanao!

"Oh, I delivered lecture-workshops and seminars on education research and statistics throughout Luzon and the Visayas, a few times in Mindanao! Well, as I'd drive my old small car to the schools here and there, a female companion or assistant would likewise be conveniently massaging all my muscles, also here and there! She was my graduate student in another state university, and she's a widow!" MAESTRO ERIMAKO tells me with pride, together with an emperor's guffaw, perhaps because of his simultaneous recall of both the folly and the pleasure. Oh, God! Here come the muscles cum massage again! I wonder why it's just all massage. Anyway, I secretly whisper to my four neurons in disgust, and oh, disappointment. Can't sex partners be more creative than that? It's getting boring for the redundancy and monotony. Oh dear, my naughty me!

"Wow, Sir! You must have been such a terrific driver, what with the overbearing intervening variable you have to contend!" I tell him matter of fact to stun him, sort of, with my now more objective listening as my ears are quite sensitized with the muscles cum massage, ejaculation, and orgasm; or his claims of superior performance! This genius, I believe needs more of the scientific listening, rather than the empathetic ear! Besides, my urinary bladders are almost exploding by now! What with my little scanty imagination that I've been trying to discipline and restrain for almost three hours of the passion, lust, and lust! The corporeal flesh is weak upon seduction, so mind power is called for especially in the company of such a brilliant and attractive septuagenarian though I just want to castrate him in my mental memoirs! I must have a fifth neuron emerging now.

"Emely, driving is like fixing her Japanese-English, typing on her portable with so much ease! Just another mechanical thing! All psychomotor coordination!" The poet behind the internationally acclaimed, "ERIMAKO'S PEN" explains rather more patiently now as he notices my confidence and newfound glory in the face of sexual radicalism, sensual affect, and moral scandal. I wonder secretly how I could also be invited by the International Poets' Society like MAESTRO ERIMAKO who's their distinguished member. "Oh, my pen is but little, and its size does not matter to the world unlike my teacher's long one!" I sadly quip to my four neurons and emerging other. "Ahh, I loved that moderating variable as I drove to lecture on all kinds of variables! My muscles were more than stimulated and prepared as they expanded and extended, helping me much to deliver more, and those lectures were well applauded! And, in between my lectures, during coffee breaks, teachers or the audience would come flaunt and flirt their wares to me. Of course, I grabbed them all. !'m a man, Emely." MAESTRO kept laughing with his shoulders while I was busy seeing the direct correlation between good sex and successful public speaking or academic lecture. I remember my good friend Charlie telling me our married female friend then sought for sex with her husband after she was lambasted by her Ateneo graduate professor for a lousy report; in her disgust, she just wanted to make love with her handsome husband so she really had to rush home; and, of course, rallied her husband to do the same, and they had the best sex ever! She eventually earned her MA in English Language and Literature Studies, but unfortunately, her handsome husband passed away. Hence, my theory is, sex can be directly proportional either to excellent public speaking or to saving one's face. Wow! Sex is hors d'oeuvre and therapy! But, who should be the partners? Morality steps in. Our friend had sex with her husband out of her frustration with her graduate program report, while MAESTRO ERIMAKO had sex repeatedly with women of all sorts!

On our third interdiscourse, same day, same restaurant, same time, oh, the same rectangular table[!], except that the restaurant manager is at the last corner table, a voluptuous cordial but quite serious woman in her forty's working on her laptop, I got the worst yet the most juicy of MAESTRO ERIMAKO'S sex escapades! Just too glad again that there was one extra table for JP and his computer games to protect his ears and innocence from the onslaught of tempestuous sex confessions by my eccentric professor that I'd later get confused if I were now a sex guru rather than a lowly biographer and memoirist.

"Emely, I also had affairs with three, to name a few, of my UP-Diliman PhD graduate students, almost at the same time. Ah, two were concurrent, literally at the same time! Two M's! Let's just call them Macky and Mildred. Macky was from Batangas, and my poem, "Taal Volcano" [included in Humor and Madness, c1997] was composed for her, a beautiful and articulate woman, look-alike of a Filipina actress (Lorna Tolentino)! The third one, just call her Nena, was from Baguio, Ilocana! All embodied a lot of pleasure! They had beautiful, flawless skin, and supple bodies!" MAESTRO laughs as if he is having a convulsion or epilepsy with his body moving like a cantankerous rustic jeepney. "Actually, Macky and Nena were at odds as they were jealous of each other!" He laughs again. "Macky was very articulate and fluent in English, so too was Nena." "Wow! It's English competence and sex!" I murmur to my four neurons. "Oh, I don't remember being classmates with them, Sir!" I tell him now trying to figure out how those female graduate students could have remained focused in his class when they were massaging their professor outside the class, perhaps in his office then? Oh, dear God, I remember so many things now that I should reserve for another memoir. Besides, I now recall stories on a white lady that frequents that corner of the UP College of Education. My God, what could she be doing there?Oh yes, in my next book!

But what really shocked me the most out of my professor's sex adventures is this one: "Do you know this actress?" He asks me. Of course, Sir! In fact, her younger sister was my student; so pretty and smart! Why do you ask, Sir? "Oh, I had an affair with their mother! She was a real sex goddess! We had a great time in bed, partaking of the carnal pleasures of stolen togetherness. I'd withdraw but she'd beg not to.

These moments were truly sexually liberating, incomparably delightful! Homer depicted human lust so well, so true, so real!" I was dumfounded, realizing how dangerous that affair was considering the popularity of the actress–daughter, and their mother's stature in the academe at that time. But, MAESTRO ERIMAKO's next confession really sent my wits out of me!

"Emely, are you aware of this congregation?" Oh, very much *po*, Sir Ed! I taught with them for sometime. Why *po*? I asked with a quivering voice, my heart palpitating. "Oh their beautiful Mother Superior, let's call her Agripina, had a big crush on me! She was my graduate student too. She'd invite me many times for dinner at their convent, with just the two of us in the dining area. She'd serve and feed me with good food, while she'd flirt with me, brushing her delicateness to my sanity. I almost made love with her right there in the convent's kitchen, but what stopped me was the chance of being found out by the other sisters and novices, and that would mean, castration of the holy women of ERIMAKO'S instrument, had they caught me and their Mother Superior in the act! But, Sr. Agripina was really a great temptation on my part as she was the most beautiful nun I have ever seen in my life, and she seemed she was then giving herself to me, wholeheartedly!"

Oh, my God! I just couldn't believe what I was hearing, so I sipped and sipped into my usual *Sago at Gulaman*. The soft tiny edible glutinous balls stuck into my straw, and I struggled to get the pressure rising so the juice could pass through and sweeten my tongue that was now filled with saliva as I was just too stunned to swallow! MAESTRO ERIMAKO gives the detailed sex adventure in vivid, specific, concrete details like what I want to read in the essays and research of my students! Is this now an overdose of the writing prompt? The genius talks of his sexual exploits like scientific experiments; precise, factual, direct to the point, logical, detailed, procedural, cold, and conclusive! Wow! This is real scientific jargon and register, and it's a genius narrating, with all his revolutionary science! Though on second thought, isn't sex really scientific because it is triggered by hormones, sensations, mindset, blood circulation, heartbeat, body fluids [I remember Ate Dulces, a biology teacher who'd talk of her sex life to us, a group of very young high school teachers then. How she'd run to the bathroom to wash away the body fluids after her terrific sex with her doctor husband! We just really had painful tummies from laughing!], of course, the sexual organs, with their respective essences---the sperm and the ovum [A female college professor was complained of by her class for drawing on the board the testicles of a man with her permanent marker! She was teaching them environmental conservation!], plus phonetic linguistics [My friend Steph, a science high school teacher shared to us, again a group of young virgin teachers that she and her Pastor husband had the best sex in their new apartment, thinking it was sound-proof, with all the segmentals and suprasegmentals of love making. The following morning, their neighbors were applauding them for their *hosannahs* and *alleluiahs*! How we fell from our chairs from incontrollable guffaws that the country's top lawyer then, who was reading his newspaper in McDo Katipunan stared at us with his threatening nonverbal legalese!] involving the two types, articulatory phonetics and acoustic phonetics, including so much paralinguistics of kinesics, kinesthetics, body movements, facial expressions, proximity [real close as in one body!];I remember how my then other close friend Cita had intimate relationship with their parish priest and who'd kiss her like Shakespeare's Romeo! But of course, they both knew it had to come to an end. Cita is now a missionary nun in Japan, so maybe she helps pray for the salvation of Kee kee's soul, and surely, the cherry blossoms and Mt. Fuji are more than thankful with the prayers, novenas, and the hymns;as well as artifacts[oh, there was this rumor on a landlady who'd satisfy her sexual appetite with her cute pink vibrator, and how her fair hands trembled in ecstasy. But, as what the nasty grapevine whispered, she was married to a much older man who obviously was long done with the carnal pleasure, that oh, she had to hire a very young and able driver to bring her to the wet market every now and then. Romance and passion indeed drive humanity to the edges. Well, to me, it's "BUWAN!" by this new band of tigers, as the song just makes me seem levitate [though, of course, that's a mortal sin!] so I just drive to about a hundred and thirty [oh, when the tires are new!] in the North Luzon Expressway, especially when I remember the tragic fate of the only man I so loved.

"Oh, by the way, she was a school administrator. She was a College Dean! But she was doing well in my graduate class, not in UP-Diliman! Her husband was filthy rich! After a few months of our affair, she told me we had to end it, or we might be both murdered! Of course, I agreed!" The confessing scientist, mathematician, philosopher, poet, educator tells me so matter of fact, without mincing words. Unbelievable!

Then, he also tells me on hindsight, "She and I reached a point that we didn't anymore mind if a baby would be conceived, but it simply wasn't meant to be! It would have been nice, if we had a Fil-Jap baby!" "Oh, quite a super baby, what with Mt. Fuji and Mayon or Taal Volcano as the conspiring godparents!" I muse to myself. This time, Sir Ed's face is as sad, but with less guilt. The Max Restaurant manager gets more than disturbed and restless, she leaves the scientist and the lowly memoirist alone, while the twelve year-old was busy with the science of technology, but the woman did not escape the flirtatious glances of MAESTRO ERIMAKO. She might have sought the comfort of the unisex toilet to unburden herself from all the succulence and striptease of a lazy afternoon, almost hearing everything her ears might have preferred than the customers': "Waiter, bill please!"

The moment I recovered from HURRICANE

ERIMAKO[!], I asked the Casanova of the hour, "so, how many women did you have, Sir?" Well, I needed the statistic to be accurate in this biographical-memoir.

"Oh, there were maybe twenty or more of them. Some were widows that enjoyed sex with ERIMAKO'S instrument! *Paano, okay naman* performance! Even now!" The controversial poet with the internationally acclaimed sexiest poem eyes me like an owl as he gives the figure. I reply: "Oh, that's quite a number, but I remember my Uncle Cleming or Clemente. He had around 150! One of them was a professor in a prestigious university along Taft…a long time ago. Maybe, I'll write his biography one day, Sir!" My voice is more than excited and steady, so the sex radical across me forgets of his flirtation. I sigh in relief, but in my mind, I wonder if he didn't get any sexually transmitted disease with all those fifteen or twenty women, single, married and widows. However, my smarter neuron tells me, he must be healthy as he is past seventy, but he can still do brisk walking, biking, and driving from Cainta to UP-Diliman. Maybe his Regression Analysis has secretly protected him all those times from the health risks of eating the forbidden fruit with different sex partners. Ah, my smarter neuron of the only four I carry in my little head quips, "He had been lucky, most of his sex partners were academicians; these people are required to have regular medical check-ups!" Just imagine a teacher of Christian Living and he's got a syphilis of the toe! My naughty neuron throws in the air, and my late husband's photo seems to shake so hard from laughter as we used to banter a lot when we were not fighting on the budget, the bills, and the chaos of life.

Finishing reading, "Humor and Madness, Jr.", I open the DZAS radio, sometime February 15 or so. The Christian Pastor is saying, "Choose trusted people who can help you reach God's dream!" My four neurons must still be drowsy from the graveyard shift of reading, "Humor and Madness" so my heart murmurs to me: "It's good to doubt. Isn't it the other day, they were airing these words: Faith is doubting your doubt!" I forget of the waiting dishes, and sit with my old floral apron on my Lorenzo's favorite resting haven, our old black and white sofa, we got on a sale in SM North, after his retirement from UP in 2013. I look up to the silent Man On The Cross. I ask him: "Am I reaching any closer to Your dream for me, writing of MAESTRO ERIMAKO'S biography?" My tears once more fall and roll, no longer on the yet to be swept and mopped forlorn tiles of our rabbit's hole, but on my tired neck, throbbing chest, and on my shivering whole being. His answer calms my misery and despair. Jesus indeed loves parables, and I'm quite thankful, I had good Theology and Literature professors! At least, I seem to understand a little of divine discourse. After washing the pair of not too fragile, not even China plates, a pair of printed and plain, small and medium sized glassware, and two old pairs of differently shaped and designed silver spoons and forks, I sit beside Kitty, peacefully eating her snacks of canned tuna and who's now fully recovering from the emergency incision I made on her chest to take out a lot of pus [but which opened chest I didn't know how to close as I lost all my sewing needles to my fury, angst, and chaos!], to save her precious, precious life [Yes, I'm now a self-discovered, self-proclaimed Vet though my PhD is Philosophy!]. My precious pen resumes work on the next episode of the MAESTRO'S life. A cold glass of water, almost full to the brim, waits nearby for intervals of print delight and penitence as I'm still human becoming [Thanks Miriam College!].

His pain is authentic. His words are painful. Sir Ed was a broken man. Yet, his brilliance kept him going. His humour saved him from the squalor and the filth of human depravity. His lust, his obliquity? Well, he was and is human, but his wisdom and propensity to the radiance of light saw him through the fulsomeness of the sex vagabond.

He writes of how his old superiors and colleagues ganged up on him; how he was ill-treated and unrewarded for meritorious work in the premier state university, where little JP used to be followed quite a lot and amazingly by the campus feline which were aplenty as we lived on the last street [JUAN LUNA ST.], with our housing unit's backyard graced by the oldest acacia in that acre and center of academic excellence. Sir Ed suffered from the hands of men and the mean side of destiny. He had to retire early at 56, but not without the battle of brave warriors; hence, the CRY of ERIMAKO! He challenged his critics, opponents, and adversaries to debates and more debates as the country's intellectuals should and must do in the midst of academic debacles, and abstrusity, including national issues to bring in the light where darkness dwells; unfortunately, they all retreated cowardly in the guise and pretense of GMRC, and resorted to shameful treacherous modus of hiding behind the carcass of those who crucified the Son of God. He was overpowered by the legion of incompetence, blindness, and rotten demagoguery. The day he walked away from the hallways of that university, more darkness fell upon Diliman, as Athena cursed the moron and the imbecility of mortals, and the young and not as young ISKOLARS NG BAYAN were deprived of that chance to learn from the only true polymath, the true, one and only one genius of the Philippines, never mind the mass, volume, and intensity of his corporeality, as who really cares among these learners when every time they walk or ride the IKOT and the TOKI in the campus, they are all but nude, with their sculpted embodiment proudly facing with open arms the approving mighty sun and when it sets, with the moon to flirt with, as stars twinkle and twinkle in obvious delight. And, should his fleshy instincts shock that center of academic freedom when the university officials and faculty suspend classes to witness the Oblation Run, together with guests, the alumni, the media, and an entire BAYAN to take a peek into the proud manhood of excited *iskolars* to run naked as they shout in all ardour and conviction their cries for social justice? Besides, the fact that he never forced Eve and her daughters to bathe with him in the sinful waters of passion and revelry.

And they hurt him. In fact, they broke his dreams. They broke his heart. MAESTRO ERIMAKO, at these crossroads in his life, wept. He wept. His tears are in his books that earned him a Guinness World Record recognition. His tears are in the internationally acclaimed poem, Dr. Cecille Velasco claims, the nastiest poem the world has ever read, "ERIMAKO'S PEN," putting him in the pedestal of poet laureates; likewise the poems "I Made a Mistake", published in the 2001 anthology *Taking Flight* by the International Library of Poetry, Owings Mills, MD, USA; and in the anthology *2001 - A Poetic Odyssey*, published by Famous Poets Society, Talent, Oregon, USA, as well as in the ILP's website; poetry. com; and "Beyond Contiguity" published in the ILP's website: poetry.com [these are in the Appendices]. But hardly does the world notice the weeping human being underneath the surface structure of those explosive verses, those naughty and witty metaphors, those lexemes, words of pun and fun. Oh, the MAESTRO is just too perfect, in that poem: overbearing yet vulnerable, invincible yet servile, satirical yet truthful. He has always been faithfully human yet incorrigibly above most homo sapiens. He cries and he triumphs; he falters yet he rises. He is the true "MONALISA"; and the world is enamored to him yet they pretend they don't. "But the works of God may be displayed in him." MAESTRO ERIMAKO, in spite of his sins is favoured by the Almighty Father, like Paul, the tax collector, and Ignatius, the sporadic offender.

The Christian Pastor over DZAS now talks of his book

but I miss its title while I blow my nose with the economical toilet tissue. I just heard, "Crossing the Jordan River," and that according to him, each one of us has to overcome our own fears to be able to cross our personal Jordan River. Like another favoured son of the Father, Moses, and the chosen people, from Egypt to the Promised Land.

Letting my little pen rest quietly on our lowly table beside Kitty's old purple cage, with her just quietly licking her three month-old lifeless front right foot, I try to reflect on my former UP professor's life; on what life he had, how he lived it, what life he has now, and how he lives it.

Ma'am Teresita, his one and only legal wife, mother of his three children [Lillian, Irma, and Eugene], has been very sick, has been very ill, is totally afflicted with an incurable brain injury. The brilliant and beautiful chemistry professor who made his world a true kaleidoscope of all the better sentiments and moments in life succumbed to such a harsh affliction; the loving wife, the doting mother, the good child of God just one day lost her health, devastating her family, most especially her husband. Sir Ed says, "She has a nurse dedicated to attend to her, 24/7." His voice is low and steady, but his face says it all, as his physics tries to compensate for the gloom that has since been enveloping him, attacking him, hurting him in all those thousands and more hours of silent grief.

Did he ever leave her? Not for long.

Did he ever abandon her? No. A big NO!

Did he ever neglect her? A resounding NO!

Does he care for her? As always!

Does he still love her?

She has always been the center and gravity of his existence, with the TRUE LIGHT nurturing and guiding this One magnificent inextinguishable fire in his heart and soul. Let's once more believe in TRUE LOVE'S FOREVER as we read his poem, "TERESITA" on the penultimate page of this PART THREE of his biography.

It's never easy to continue facing life, hurdling its ordeals pursuing excellence, achieving on top of the world, raising three children alone, giving them the best education, helping them to their dreams, plus teaching so many students, mentoring here and there, "lawyering" (giving legal advice and writing legal pleadings) for colleagues, friends, and even an entire nation, maintaining friendships, writing and producing the best books, developing novel, brilliantly innovative paradigms [VPA Model], when the beloved is beyond all possible cure to be just like old times. But he did it.

Indeed, Sir Ed did it. In all those years of his brokenness, of suffering, of loneliness, of injustice and persecution, of ennui and emptiness, of frailty and vulnerability, of sin and grave sin--he just did it.

"TAKE A STEP OF FAITH!" Again the Christian Pastor over DZAS admonishes.

Sir Ed took it in the face of great adversity. He dared cross his Jordan River. He was but frightened, seeing such invidious, sinister, and ominous life, but he gave his ONE GOOD FIGHT [*KUNG HINDI AKO, SINO? KUNG HINDI NGAYON, KAILAN?*] The light never left him as he crossed the formidable river, with audacious inveteracy, with the talents and skills he knew he has, with that hope which perched upon his heart, with that beautiful faith his science finds no principle nor theory to explain, but the OMNIPOTENCE, GREATNESS, AND PROVIDENCE of his God.

But it did not come easy. It was never a walk in the sweet valleys and prairies of life. Crossing the Jordan River almost, almost drowned him, and he almost submitted to the depth and rage of the river. But the light persisted. The light prevailed.

"For thou has delivered my soul from death, mine eyes from tears, and my feet from falling."[Psalm 116:8]

"My life in UP was very stressful." Sir Ed speaks the words in such intensity of emotion. I keep my silence. JP continues to play his computer games on my old laptop on the other nearby table. This time, most rectangular tables are getting occupied. Max's Restau is now a lot busier and full. Time, as ever is unmindful and in haste.

"It was in 1984 that my wife started to get sick. That was also the time I got the British Council Fellowship Grant. It was a very difficult period of my life. I had to make a very difficult decision, to leave her in the care of my mother, of my family. And the kids were still very young. But I knew I had to go to London." His eyes bring him back to those tough times; they blink and look with the dagger of a yesterday.

His extramarital affairs, especially with KeeKee, a Japanese, seemed the man's attempts to escape the tragedy of his marriage. I don't know, I'm not sure, and who am I to know? Sir Ed tells me of how he experienced culture shock and language shock on his first weeks in London. He was tied there for about ten months of postgraduate studies. He felt he was all alone, the alienation and the angst got him. KeeKee was also suffering the same. All the Orientals, the Asians, all the foreign students suffered the same in that great country, one of the coldest regions on Earth. But Sir Ed's burden seemed so much more than any other as he left a very sick wife, and three minor children in the Philippines. "It must have been damningly debilitating and truly, a heavy cross to bear." I find the words in my heart. Every human suffering afflicts and inflicts the human heart, for each and everyone gets wounded by life, at one point or in more times of our mortal existence. We all know how these wounds can hurt, hurt so bad, hurt too deeply, hurt endlessly. No one is exempted; no one is spared. The wounds may just come in different forms at different periods of human life. As Shakespeare wrote, that men die a thousand times here on Earth. Sir Ed was besieged by such wounds persistently in so many years. Yet, he didn't give up. He persevered in the midst of his ordeals, in the face of all his sins. The light did not forsake him though he was trekking the path to nothingness, to the horrifying depths of sin. God acted on his behalf. "The sorrows of death compassed me, and the pains of hell got hold upon me: I found trouble and sorrow. Then called I upon the name of the Lord; O Lord, I beseech thee, deliver my soul. Gracious is the Lord and righteous: yea, our God is merciful."[Psalm 116:3-5].

Sir Ed's affair with KeeKee lasted three years. His guilt was great at the beginning. It was just passion and desire at the start. He'd travel to Japan three times in a year. And, he had other affairs with all those other women, single, married, and widows. Yes, Sir Ed became a callous man in the vixen and bosom of sin; he was, indeed, in a lot of wretchedness. He led then a sinful life. Yet, he just kept going. He just kept nurturing his God-given talents. While he faltered, he kept improving himself. "I shall not die but live, and declare the works of the Lord."[Psalm 118:17]

But, if we read into the lives of many saints, isn't MAESTRO ERIMAKO'S life [of his London and Japan exploits, plus his sex adventures in the Philippines], similar? The sins may be in different faces and phases, but don't we see the common denominator? Human frailty! THE SINS COMMITTED BY A HUMAN BEING. But, yet, the beautiful common denominator, THE SINNER JUST KEPT GOING, IMPROVING HIMSELF ALONG THE WAY.

Sir Ed had to take on many jobs to send his three children to school. Aside from teaching then in UP, he also worked for Ilocos Sur Assemblyman, Salacnib Baterina, [his DWCV college accounting classmate] as his research staff at the Batasang Pambansa, and even tutored the Assemblyman's eldest, Celia;

this job he assumed while pursuing his PhD also in UP-Diliman. The late Dr. Alfonso Pacquing invited him then to join the line-up of faculty in the Department of Educational Administration, right after one academic semester of enrolling in the same department for his doctorate. And, while juggling these jobs and his doctoral studies, he was also tending to his very sick wife, and their children. Listening to my professor as he opens so many doors and windows of his personal life to me, I can just admire the man for his perseverance, diligence, tenacity, intelligence, hard work, selflessness, and sacrifice.

"Yes, I taught for twenty-two years in UP. It was really a very stressful life for me. I'd go home to Vigan, Ilocos Sur, once a month to visit my family." Sir Ed once more makes the emphatic recollection, but I do not sense any regret, neither repulsion; just simply the exhaustion, very normal to each and everyone who takes not just one job, but several others, moonlighting here and there, in between doing good and falling into sin, yet striving for the greater things in life, for more that life could offer.

But with the deluge of intellectual bias and prejudice, that deprived him to do more and become more in the premier state university, Sir Ed knew his mission there had ended. He opted to retire early in 2001 from the university. He then joined the roster of faculty of other state universities: the Technological University of the Philippines [TUP], in Manila; Bulacan State University, in Malolos; Philippine State College of Aeronautics, in Pasay City; and even University of the East, in Manila. At the same time, he also worked as a Department of Education (DepEd) and UNESCO consultant, the latter for a short stint New Delhi, India, in particular; but as a Research and Statistics Consultant for both agencies. He also gave seminar-workshops on research and statistics mostly all over Luzon and the Visayas. All these jobs and responsibilities he took upon his shoulders as Lillian, Irma, and Eugene went to their respective schools to pursue their own dreams. Sir Ed's and Ma'am Teresita's children chased their dreams in the same passion and excellence as their parents had earlier on done. Lillian, with her BS and MS in Chemistry was absorbed as faculty of UP-Diliman's College of Science, Chemistry Department, until she decided to become a full-time homemaker. Irma is now a Doctor of Medicine from UP-Manila, a radiologist, who works for several hospitals in Metro Manila, mainly in Medical City, Pasig. She earned her undergraduate degree in Chemistry also from UP-Diliman, just like her older sister. And again, just like Lillian, she taught at the Department of Chemistry, also in UP Diliman, College of Science. Both the two daughters of Sir Ed followed their mom's footsteps of studying the chemicals, substances, and elements of this world. Eugene, an ECE engineer, the product of his father's experiment, now works as a navigation engineer for a French-Norwegian oil exploration ship. He earned his Electronics and Communications Engineering at TUP, Manila. All three children of Sir Ed are now happily married to their equally brilliant and professional spouses, and their respective kids are all excelling in Math and Science, even in Taekwondo and Gymnastics. The eldest grand-daughter of Sir Ed, Mikaela, is all set to Stanford University for a possible degree in Aeronautics Engineering. She's at the same time a member of the Philippine National Taekwondo Team, Cadet Division, [with Gold and Bronze medals, aside from Math and Science]. Eunice and Elyssia are recent SEA-DEPED Math and Science Excellence awardees, aside from being YES Awardees, also in Math and Science, same as their much younger cousins, Ima, Leona, and Eoghan, all medalists too. Elyssia is an excellent gymnast. She recently bagged the title, that of the All Around Champion in the recently concluded 2019 Philippine Cup, and her SPCP TEAM, as the Second Place Team Champion. Elyssia has been winning medals in gymnastics, like in the 2018 Philippine Cup Competition, bringing home five medals.

Looking into the lives and achievements of Sir Ed's children, with their respective families, anyone would say that their father raised them well, and not just well; ON TOP OF THE LINE. CREAM OF THE CROP.

Who are we then to condemn him for his faults and sins? Listening today again to my favorite radio station, with its program, Family Matters [of Maru Javier and Avelyn Garcia], talking and sharing on how God overlooks our faults because of His love, proceeding from the biblical, "The greatest is love," "Anyone who says he loves me but does not love his neighbour is a liar", and capping their discourse on the five languages of love [quality time, physical touch, gift-giving, acts of service, words of affirmation], with the poem, "If Only I Knew," I can only look at myself, into my own life, upon all my burdens and difficulties, and answer this question: What have I been doing in the face of such adversities, of such ordeals? A rhetorical question inspired by MAESTRO ERIMAKO'S life.

"*Sige, pray muna tayo…*" Sir Ed sends me this text message six minutes after one o'clock in the afternoon on February 27, 2019 [This was the day I finished drafting his biography].

"Yes *po*, Sir Ed!" I reply with my heart gladdened, by the gifts of life and love of such a man who takes a Japanese-sounding man's first name to match then the first name of his Japanese paramour or concubine, but who went on to bring this seminally sinful pseudonym to the top of the world as a Guinness World Record author's nom de plume. His inner strength, through all those times of sin and pain, a love so true that remained fixed in his faith, his love for the chemistry professor he married after one year from his college graduation, and that time, I was five years old, almost his favorite even digit, SIX. So, I pray with his poem of that wonderful love:

TERESITA

T'was a quick quirk and flourish of serendipity,
Ever and forever alive and afire in my heart.
Reexamine I did my schooling's locus and focus.
Erelong the hand of Destiny guided a change of---
Sight; from stoic accounting to affective teaching.
In no time you appeared as the be-all and end-all:
That posthaste set my heart aflame and afire.
Again, if I have to do it again, I would, Teresita!
Eduardo Jr. [February 2019]

Oh, how my heart and soul yearn to do the same, to express my prayer through a poem for my fallen beloved, my husband, the late LORENZO QUIAMBAO ORILLOS. And so, my song in a poem of prayerful love:

My tears just keep falling and rolling
     To wheresoever
          But hoping they reach him
               Who now sleeps in eternal silence
                Not to burden his repose
     Just to let him know
       I still remember
          The only man
                    Who loved me.
                    [his widow, EBO 2019]

"THE GREATEST OF ALL THESE
IS LOVE" [1 Corinthians 13:13]

PART FOUR
GLORIOUS SCIENCE IN THE MADNESS OF HIS PEN

HUMORING THE UNIVERSE

Is a man of reason also a man of faith?
Is a sexy mind also in a state of grace?
Is the humor of Alicias also the humor of the universe?
Is he therefore a child of God?
Or, is he more a child of Science?

Sometime in February 2019, Sir Ed sent me an email: "That's the front cover of my latest book...soon to be published. I disputed the works of the beacons of scholarship across history... including David Hume, Karl Popper, and great professors of Harvard University, University of California (Los Angeles & San Diego), University of North Carolina, Stanford University, Johns Hopkins University, University of the Philippines, etc."

I was doing the dishes that waited overnight to be washed, attending to my cat, Kitty, whose one leg has been declared lifeless by my late husband's favorite Vet. My floral apron was dripping wet as the faucet was uncontrollably pumping out so much water; maybe my godmother Queen Fairy of my little Indian war girl days wanted everything to be quick, fast and easy considering that I've been widowed for almost two years, getting my hands full, depriving me of leisure and pleasure. Well, Sir Ed's front cover looked quite tempting so I hastily removed my wet delicate comfort, and threw myself on the waiting sofa that still smells very well of my Lorenzo up to this time of sporadic interdiscourses with ERIMAKO'S pen.

Wow! Explosively bombastic! Sir Ed never misses to excite both the flesh and the mind, never mind the spirit? His instrument is very cute, at least to me whose pigeon hole in that university in Loyola Heights never was occupied by such an amazing object of matter. Oh, is that a sophisticated telescope protruding on his front? But I forgot to ask my professor as he started to pour his incredibly juicy, oozing, and meaty morning delight before my naked eyes. I screamed in awe and wanton pleasure while I got the feel of Sir Ed's, my gosh, firm and vigorous two-pronged, two-headed stand and stance to my now unquenchable desire for more and more and so much more: a lighthouse and a ground telescope.

His science is first class! I was overpowered. Mind over matter, indeed. Then my *celfone* vibrated as it never did before. Sr. Mary Celine Santos, SPC, just sent me a text message: "Thank God! Praise the Lord! As ever, put all your TRUST in God's hands!" I was dumbfounded. How science and faith worked together for me that February morning.

On our second interdiscourse face to face, he gave me, oh, his two cents. "Finally, I can touch his front cover, especially his instrument!" I secretly mused to my eager self. Oh, it's in black and white, classic! But, truly, more than an hors d'oeuvre; it's an irresistible main course for anyone who's sick and tired of the usual intelligence---rigid, self-serving, too premature. Oh, Sir Ed's latest book, though still in press (off the press on

13 March 2019), offers so much stimulating foreplay of science, math, and statistics, language learning and neurolinguistics, presidential and the parliamentary forms of government, including teacher evaluation and student classroom cognitive performance. He titled this exceptionally radical, intriguing but brilliantly enlightening book as "The Epigone's Two cents Versus The Beacon's Five Cents." Is it a farce or satire that he has on the front cover, or analogous to classical thought vis-à-vis a sexy mind, oh revolutuionary and titillating? "Huh, Sir Ed, here come the frills of our private jokes in between our disjunct [Thanks Dr. Dita!] coffee breaks!" I laughed in self-abandon as the insipid thoughts and moments of my existence had to take a backseat to give way to an exuberant science, and oh well, to some green, greener, too green [Good Lord!] jokes of the genius as his scientific discourse is always laced with his second skin—his sensual, emotive, textured, and oh, super bombastic fleshy humor.

Applying induction and deduction, trying to think Humean or Popperian [Oh popcorn!], I asked the universe while driving myself and my twelve- year old son through the neck of another Saturday traffic, how this genius of a Filipino came to his peak, and how he continues to toy with all possible fields of human knowledge. Was he ever human from the start? Is there sufficient evidence for his more human side? His genius is a given.

While I got the lowest mark in his class in 1984, as a twenty year old M.Ed. student in UP, I feel I also learned with my sneakers, colourful socks, denim skirts and bright colored blouses, maybe psychologically, as a way of compensating then for my feeble, daydreaming intellect [wondering if my professor was a demigod of both lush green agriculture of rounds and oblongs, and rationality] among smart and self-confident school principals and sophisticated university officials, with me, a neophyte high school teacher of English and Journalism in St.

Mary's College, Quezon City, under the very competent and motherly coordinatorship of my dearest *ninang*, the beautiful, articulate, and elegant Antonietta "Nonette or Net" Corpuz.

I started to research and ask around on the humanity of the genius. Of course, I sought Sir Ed's competent and able help to save on cost and optimize benefit, output, and outcome. His closest and brilliant students came to my rescue, and gave me all kinds of data, quanti- and quali-, first hand or not much, personal or vicarious, seen or felt, experienced or heard, skewed or direct, part or whole, truth or truthful. Hence, the empirical data matrix of the more human side of the Who's Who In The World, the holder of a Guinness World Record Award, the Distinguished Member of the International Poets' Society, one of Outstanding People of the 20th Century [get also the 21st Sir!], the International Biography recognition, and many more. And now, the Grecian lyre and violin usher in a world of the most beautiful words and memories of grateful, successful former students for their great professor, of the sexiest mind so far in the now borderless world, which seems to float like one big atom in a bubble. Let's all take the delightful revelry of remembering ALL THOSE CRAZY AND GOOD TIMES IN THE LIFE OF A LIVING FILIPINO GENIUS. He's remembered as follows:

Sir Ed: A Man for All Seasons

I came to know Professor Eduardo R. Alicias Jr. when he became my Science teacher when I was in 4th year high school in Divine Word College of Vigan.

At that time, I was not very interested with my studies because studying well would hamper my 'happy go-lucky' life style. I thought then that '*Wastong pag-aaral ay nakakasira sa barkadahan*.' However, that naughty foolish thinking gradually vanished every time that I attended the science classes of Sir Ed,

His mastery of science, teaching it in a very interesting way, giving practical examples that an elementary student could understand, injecting [injection was his favorite up to now] humor along the way and occasionally giving inspirational talks in and out of his science classes, specially to students like me, struck me to my very core. He is an educator through and through. Unlike other teachers that in their classes sleeping is better than listening, in Sir Ed's you feel alive. You don't even want the bell to ring so that you could go home. For me he is not only a good teacher. He feels the pulse of people, students or otherwise, their sadness, joy and other sentiments. He is very human that's why he is one of my best friends from my '*buanger*' high school days in Vigan up to my present mellowing years. As a true BFF, he never never leaves a friend hanging in the air no matter what…a very rare quality of a man.

In Sir Ed's younger years, he chose to teach in a Catholic school. He even taught at the Vigan Minor Seminary before he became a professor of UNP, then UP. I assumed that he is a devoted Catholic, God fearing and a law abiding citizen. While he did not teach a Rizal subject in school, Sir Ed is a Filipino in every sense of it. Offers for him to teach abroad were all refused by him. Why? He wanted to share his God-given talents to us Filipinos. He is a principled man. He might not have written a NOLI or FILI, for it is no longer timely to Filipinos at this present time, but nevertheless has written books on science, education, government analysis, joke, etc. etc. etc. for the whole universe to read; and in so doing, the peoples of the world will realize that a Filipino genius, a man for all seasons exists here in the Philippines in the person of Professor Eduardo R. Alicias Jr. ----**ATTY. FELIX RACADIO, VIGAN, ILOCOS SUR**

EDUARDO R. ALICIAS, JR., "THE LAWYER"

I often and fondly call him, Sir Ed. He is an excellent researcher, mathematician/statistician, author of several published books across varying disciplines, e.g., on education, political science, development economics, public administration, etc., and a profound thinker. He is a Guinness World Record holder—for the longest preface relative to the main body of the book [Humor and Madness, c1997, ISBN 971-91402-3-2]. He is intelligent, analytic, logical, creative, and poetic; he's author of several published poems, humorous and/or romantic. Yes, he is a man of great humor and/or romance. Moreover, he's a de facto lawyer—writing legal pleadings as does a licensed lawyer *de campanilla*. He has written a number of successful legal pleadings [e.g., complaints and counter affidavits] for and in my behalf—coherent, well argued, grounded on facts & legal provisions and doctrines, and laced with supporting items in jurisprudence [Supreme Court decisions]. I know for a fact that his "client" won a case at the Civil Service Commission and then at the Court of Appeals—versus a true-blue licensed *de campanilla* lawyer. Indeed, I am really lucky to have been a friend of Sir Ed. This guy is simply amazing!--**FRANCIS ALFARO, ASST. PROFESSOR & FORMER MEMBER, BOARD OF REGENTS [BOR], TECHNOLOGICAL UNIVERSITY OF THE PHILIPPINES [TUP]**

The Mighty Pen of Eduardo R. Alicias, Jr.; The VPA

I am Aurelio P. Ramos Jr. ["Jun"], founder and Principal of the Berea Arts and Sciences High School located in Cainta, Rizal. My discipline is mathematics. My teaching experience includes teaching mathematics and computer science at the College of Science, University of the Philippines, Diliman, Quezon City;

mathematics at the Ateneo de Manila University High School, Quezon City; and mathematics and computer science at the La Salle Greenhills, Mandaluyong City.

Teaching mathematics to junior high school students intrigued me, so earlier on I shifted direction and concentration to mathematics education where I'd find it more fulfilling. I founded the Berea Arts and Sciences High School in 2005, a very unique high school—combining in its curriculum, the rigors of math and the sciences and the aesthetics of arts and music. So far, I am seeing admirable outcomes of the first batches of graduates who underwent our curriculum. I am very proud of such outcomes in our student-graduates.

To further equip me with education, I took Curriculum and Instruction as my PhD program, and worked on Curriculum Evaluation as my dissertation. Unfortunately, I didn't finish it because I got sick, and had to be medically observed for some years. When I was cleared by my doctor, I went back to school, but this time taking a course on Industrial Education Management.

I am now working on my dissertation, and I have chosen to work on the theory/model of Eduardo R. Alicias Jr. on "Variance Partitioning Analysis [VPA]". I see in the VPA a sense of novelty and seminality. As I see it, as I understand its simple yet profound elegance—after months of struggling and grappling with its internal logic and stern beauty—I feel something orgasmic to the point that I dare verbally ejaculate, thus: the discovery and/or invention of the VPA appears analogous, at least to me, to Einstein's relativity theory subsuming and superseding Newton's deterministic formulations of the physics of gravity and motion. To use a metaphor, the VPA appears to be tectonic-shaking, sort of, in the philosophical and/or methodological substratum of educational research and evaluation. It intrigues and excites me a lot that this VPA can indeed blossom into something realistically applicable and useful in the field of education. Hence, it's not surprising that my chosen doctoral research topic/title is: "Evaluating Objectively Teacher Performance Using Variance Partitioning Analysis [VPA]". My objective is to test and experience, probably for the first time, the practical application or feasibility of the VPA to objectively evaluate teacher performance.

The topic becomes more sanguinely interesting to me, since I personally know the person [Ed Alicias, the VPA father] who seminally formulated and proposed the VPA in a peer reviewed journal **[see Education Policy Analysis Archives, Volume 13, Number 30, May 6, 2005, ISSN 1068-2341; Arizona State University and University of South Florida]**. We were dormmates [Narra Residence Hall] at the University of the Philippines, Diliman, in the early eighties, while we were doing our graduate studies in separate fields, I occasionally consulted him on how to conduct my undergraduate statistics class in another university. Through the years I have discussed and even argued with him about research methods and related statistical tools used in conducting research and/or analyzing data. Indeed, in a nontrivial sense, I do say that since then he has acted as my mentor in these fields all these years.- ---**AURELIO P. RAMOS JR., FOUNDER AND PRINCIPAL, BEREA ARTS AND SCIENCES HIGH SCHOOL, CAINTA, RIZAL; FORMER FACULTY, COLLEGE OF SCIENCE, UP-DILIMAN.**

Note: A brilliant discussion on the VPA MODEL by Prof Aurelio "Jun" P. Ramos Jr. is presented in the Appendices hereof.

The Young Dr. Ed: School Principal, Chess Tactician

Humble, brilliant and filled with possibilities. I met Dr. Ed 44 years ago in my freshman year in high school, a very young principal in our exclusive school for young men with vocations. He's a calculating mathematician both in theory and life. Riding a bicycle to work, he's a believer and practitioner of 'sound mind in a sound body', focused and prepared, always making difficult formulas easy for everyone's comprehension. There was no wrong answer for Dr. Ed; he's always leading the confused to the right answer. Many among us who did not find that vocation were inspired by his brilliance, followed him in UP after he resigned and pursued a more significant career. A chess tactician, who I can still recall gave Argentinian grandmaster Quinteros a hard time winning, left alone face to face with him after downing 50 other chess wannabe grandmasters in Ilocos Sur. He lifted our school standard, even as a young principal with his excellence in math.

In my recall, none ever matched his dedication, creativity, and the pursuit of excellence as principal in our school.—**DR. GERRY TOLENTINO, M.D., CANDON. ILOCOS SUR**

Dr. "Atty." Ed Alicias: Our Legal Guru

Dr. Ed Alicias is an excellent paralegal adviser. He knows the law [almost all areas], and he excels at writing pleadings and enabling you to win legal cases. I was once the President of the Faculty Association and Federation of Faculty Associations, Technological University of the Philippines [TUP]. We fought hard for our recognition at the Department of Labor and Employment [DOLE], Civil Service Commission [CSC], Public Sector & Labor Management Council [PSLMC], and in other government agencies.

In those battles, Dr. "Atty" Ed was our legal adviser. There were instances when we had to go to the Department of Justice, Court of Appeals, and even at the Supreme Court. It was worth the experience because we had Dr. "Atty" Alicias advising us on what to do and how to go about it. We won in a number of our legal battles because he wrote for us, and provided us with legal knowledge on: labor laws, civil code, graft and corruption, civil service laws, among others. He translated our concerns for justice and equity into well argued and well written pleadings; thus inspiring and empowering us to face and vanquish our legal adversaries.

Indeed, if you are his friend, he will stand by your side without expecting anything in return. He is so passionate in lawyering for us—so much so that even at midnight, upon the flash of an inspiration or dream, he wouldn't hesitate to rise up from bed just to refine and rewrite the draft of a legal pleading. I/we can't thank him enough. Nonetheless, I say yet again:

Thank You, to a GREAT MAN OF MANY TALENTS, prolific and profound, laced with a lot of humor!"----**DR. JULIET A. CATANE, DEAN, COLLEGE OF LIBERAL ARTS, TECHNOLOGICAL UNIVERSITY OF THE PHILIPPINES [TUP]**

"You rubbed off some of that genius mind on your student"

You are such a great mentor and teacher. I would not have made it this far had you not entrusted to me, some of your precious and unique ideas. You rubbed off some of that genius mind on your student. Where this **Al** will go as far as research is concerned, it always has shadows of that great mentor I had…**Al…icias**. Thanks Sir. I've always been looking at patterns from you silently. You, Sir…are the bigger neuron…I am a sullen prototype of a miniscule neuron following your footsteps.---**Unsolicited Comments from DR. AL CAO, AUTHOR/PROFESSOR, UPLB graduate, Professor, BULACAN STATE UNIVERSITY**

My Fond Recollections of Dr. Eduardo R. Alicias Jr.

Sir Ed was our intelligent principal and science teacher at the Immaculate Conception Minor Seminary, then Municipality of Vigan, from 1971 to 1975 [for our batch]. Being a poor young man then [he narrated to us once he went to primary school with his pair of worn out slippers], he came to teach in the seminary riding on his *beinte ocho* [28-inch rim] bicycle whose tire one day was deflated obnoxiously by a naughty seminarian. Career-driven, he enrolled in master's studies. I often saw him during his lunch breaks preparing his requirements or anayzing chess moves, for he, together with his brother, Robert, was a well-known chess player and champion in the province during those years.

We crossed paths again at the University of the Philippines, Diliman, Quezon City in 1988 when I had my graduate studies there. Sir Ed was then a professor at the College of Education. I learned from him that when he finished his master's studies, he taught at our school in Vigan, the University of Northern Philippines for one year. Then, he went to UP for his doctoral studies in 1978. After his studies, he was absorbed by the college as a professor. I still remember what he told me once that he pursued his studies for the sake of his children. Of course, his two daughters graduated from UP, not because of his intervention but because of his and his wife's superior genes. They are as brilliant as their parents are.

We were dorm-mates at the famous now burned down Narra Residence Hall. He used to tag me along to PCED Hotel restaurant where he would meet and exchange humor and madness, as well as cerebral blows, with his fellow intellectuals, like Arnold Molina Azurin, another famous and brilliant Ilocano from Vigan. How I admired them!

In my dissertation, Sir Ed was my informal adviser and statistician as I was enrolled at the then College of Public Administration. There are two priceless lessons he imparted to me, to wit: writing theoretical framework and related literature and understanding the basics of regression analysis. They are lifelong learnings which I have used conveniently and effectively in my advising and during panel presentations until very recently.

Concerning the first, he taught me to start with the box of dependent variable (DV) by defining the concept as considered by experts and in books, followed by how researchers had operationalized the concept, then by how I, as the researcher, interpret and/or wish to operationalize the concept. He then taught me to interpret the arrow between the DV box and the IV box as a transition, a conjectured causal bridge from the independent variable (IV) box. For instance, using pupil performance as DV, he taught me to state something like this: pupil performance is thought of to be a function of several variables, such as individual factors, e.g., IQ, study habits, etc. and school factors, e.g., teacher competence, etc. Then proceed similarly, for instance, "teacher competence." Define it as experts and books had considered the concept. Then show how studies had operationalized it and/or how I propose to operationalize it. After having done that, Sir Ed told me, I have already constructed my own theory, i.e., my own set of hypothesized relationships.

With respect to the second, he advised me to read, say, the book of Fred Kerlinger on multivariate analysis. We did the data analysis of my dissertation at his house for overnight without sleep. After the printout is done, he taught me how to prepare the tables and interpret the analytical results. I had learned because I had an exceptional mentor. I could advise graduate students effectively and argue with fellow professors convincingly on matters of research and statistical analysis, particularly regression analysis, because Sir Ed taught me how.

Sir Ed is also a lawyer, *de facto*. In a sexual harassment complaint of a female faculty member in a state university against the President, he acted as the "Atty. Alicias" whom the complainant never met in person. He and the complainant transacted legal business (lawyer-client transaction) only through a common friend. The President on the other hand, hired the services of a very prominent *de campanilla* lawyer as legal counsel. The pleadings that Sir Ed wrote demolished convincingly the respondent's answer/defense, and the complainant won her case, initially at the Civil Service Commission, and on respondent's appeal, at the Court of Appeals. The president was properly punished. With respect to the litigation of the civil case involving his farm in Vigan, he sought the assistance of a licensed lawyer. However, he himself wrote the pleadings. And, his counsel was awed. They won the case, both at the RTC and at the Court of Appeals. His Erimako's Farm, at the heart of the city, now measuring 1.6 hectares, boasts of grown up gmelina trees and fruit trees, e.g., calamansi, guyabano, pomelo, jackfruit, etc. Likewise, it contains a promenade that also serves as function hall cum self-designed clay statues of peeing Erimako and his peeing beautiful Salvacion, mini swimming pools cum fountains, and bamboo & palm cottages—all designed by "Engineer" Ed Alicias. Thus, he comes home to Vigan occasionally to visit his farm. There are many more legal cases that he himself handled---from disbarment of lawyers, prosecutors, and a judge/justice to questioning the constitutionality of the language provision of K-12 program. A non-lawyer and without formal schooling in law, his pleadings have reached the Supreme Court. In all of these, he acted as a "Pro Se"--representing himself in any type of legal or court action without the benefit of a licensed legal counsel.

Because of Sir Ed's outstanding accomplishments in the field of education, the University of Northern Philippines, his former employer, accorded him the award "Outstanding Ilocano Educator" during its 2005 foundation anniversary.

When I availed of the sabbatical leave in our university in 2017, I was required to do research and have it published in a refereed journal. Sir Ed readily offered his services to do the statistical analyses. He also reviewed my questionnaire and suggested to include as an item--sex as a motivation for tourists to visit a place. Of course, this is suggestive of the prurient and libidinous side of Dr. Alicias the elaboration of which I leave to others to do.

He has two publicly admitted passions in life, reading and writing. He has authored several books copies of which he has shared to me. He is a prolific as well as fertile writer.

Sir Ed is also a true friend. When I had the difficulty of going home, he offered me wholeheartedly his newly built cottage.

Indeed, it has been an honor and privilege of being a student, town mate, dorm-mate, informal advisee, and friend of Sir Ed. He has been an incessant source of wisdom and inspiration, May there be more Sir Ed!"---
-DR. FERDINAND LAMARCA, FORMER VICE-PRESIDENT, UNIVERSITY OF NORTHERN PHILIPPINES [UNP], VIGAN, ILOCOS SUR

MY PROFESSOR, MY IDOL

Totoong Tao! Maginoo pero medyo bastos! He's a good professor whose depth is that of a genius! He specializes in a lot of fields, but he is fondest of regression analysis. He loves pointing out myths and fallacies in his narrations and anecdotes. His choice of words defeats those of opposing lawyers and/or writers. Only that he was the most misunderstood professor of Bulacan State University (BSU) for he is so green, so fond of green jokes! Only those who are, well, smart can understand and appreciate him. *Hindi siya kayang intindihin ng mababaw na tao.* He's the Einstein of the Philippines! In spite of his green mind, he is a very principled man. University of the Philippines (UP) lost so much when they let go of him that early. *Wala siyang kapantay!*— **AN INTERVIEW WITH DR. DANNY HILARIO, FORMER PROFESSOR, VICE-PRESIDENT, AND REGENT, BULACAN STATE UNIVERSITY**

REMINISCENCES ABOUT DR. EDUARDO R. ALICIAS, JR.
"The Einstein of His Generation"

I couldn't exactly remember how I started befriending Dr. Ed. As far as I know, I met him when I was in my early 20's, during my Master of Education schooling days at Technological University of the Philippines [TUP] in Manila. He was and until now a nasty type of professor who was/is fond of cracking "dirty jokes"..at least for me [a typical young *probinsyana* from Laguna] who is not used to "green jokes". I was always pissed off with his analogy of women's breast to his lecture on skewness in statistics--because at that time, I was the subject of his comparison, indeed, attention. Good God, I got engineer-classmates who kept me calm during his lectures, and who would tell me it's just a joke. Anyway, I got a 1.25 grade, despite my negative thoughts and/or words about him.

I just knew him well during my doctorate days when he offered himself as my dissertation adviser. I was very hesitant to accept his proposal because of his "foul-mouthed" expressions. However, due to his "Einstein" ways of teaching and thinking, I began to appreciate his views in and about life, his overwhelming ideas and knowledge of everything under the sun. He was/is the type of person who will never accept defeat in an argument. He always won every time we argued about my dissertation.

I was very glad I graduated with the degree, Doctor of Education despite his "short tempered" ways of advising every time I consulted with him on my dissertation research. Dr. Ed is also a typical Ilokano who is known for being "kuripot". During my dissertation writing days, I couldn't get much discount from his professional fee; he values much every single centavo he earned from his work such as consultation, doing statistical analysis, advising, editing, among others. A very "wise spender" guy I've known.

One of the best things I got from Dr. Ed was that he never left me when I was in the midst or brink of giving up during the oral defense of my dissertation. He pinned down panel members who questioned my results, and abashed them with "a number of authors" in statistics I never heard of or known in my lifetime, debating over my results. Good God, I didn't give birth at that precise time; I was at that time in my ninth month of pregnancy of twins.

With that incident, I found him to be a good natured-man, a man of principles and unfathomable philosophies in life. I've known him for almost 30 years. I would say, that the man is such a man with "beautiful mind"..the "Einstein" of his generation. His brilliant discourse over things trivial or of the utmost importance shows that he has always something to say about it, either using "obnoxious" illustrations, paradigm, or instances."

Dr. Ed has so much to give to the world…, his expertise in any subject of your choice. He's an author, an erudite researcher, and a bogus lawyer [lol]; he's damn good in writing court pleadings, an amazing skill for a non-law graduate. What Dr. Ed couldn't be or do? I couldn't think of anything he can't.

As a friend and former student of Dr. Ed, I would say I was very lucky for knowing him and for being friends until now. Despite our 2 decades age gap, I learned to accept his "unusual" ways of conversation, and "green jokes" [that's his nature] every time we chat or text. Most of his acquaintances are also my acquaintances, maybe because of Facebook and seminars attended. There's no seminar or conference I have attended where some participants don't know him [popular huh?], and most of them have the same remarks. "Dr. Ed? he's very fond of beautiful woman, natural Casanova" of his time.

One of the best books he has ever written is "Humor and Madness" which depicts his real nature and personality. The nastiest poem ever written which received worldwide acclaim, "ERIMAKO'S PEN", has been read by many including myself.

Until now we communicate; he is still my mentor, editor [best writer, though sometimes I don't understand his language with indecipherable meaning [lol], adviser, and lawyer or [liar? hahaha], consultant, statistician and a father sometimes.

…the sweetest words I heard from him? "good, *nag-improve ka na*, you are learning..from me."---**DR. CECILLE VELASCO, PROFESSOR AND HEAD OF ALUMNI AFFAIRS, LAGUNA STATE POLYTECHNIC UNIVERSITY**

> Greatness in Humility.
> Humility in Greatness.
> Overwhelming Numbers!
> Overwhelming Science!
> What Thought!
> Overwhelming Grace!
>> Alicias, Jr. E. is Eduardo Alicias, Jr.
>> Aristotle's A is A.
>> He is two in one.
>> Human and More Than Human!
> My little pen hesitates…
> My head swirls…
>> I begin to doubt my words…
>> Why did I offer to write of this genius?
>> But I remember the balls and the eggplants,
>> My lowly pen is tickled, and the words come again.

ALICIAS, JR., E. IS JUST TOO SEXY
FOR MY PEN! –EBO 2019

Wow! Hearing and reading of such compliments and praises, fun and affectionate tales and anecdotes on the man who continues to put the Philippines in the frontiers of human knowledge just made me appreciate more his humanity, well, even his inevitable sexy humor that can really be blatant in most times—objectionable or offensive to the more conservative ears, to the traditionalists, and to the hard core moralists. Yet, this genius is a lot more than the sexy mind of science, numbers, and reason. He has a good heart, and it is a good one. He loves humanity that's why he keeps on searching for more in the universe though sometimes he says, "I want to forget the world once in a while." His exquisite brilliance is dedicated to the truth as he is faithful to his God-given mission—to contribute selflessly to the illumination, enlightenment, and prosperity of everyone, especially those he encounters and interacts with, or interdiscourses. Knowledge to him, I surmise, is the key to a life of bliss and contentment. I see Herman Hesse's Sidhartha in this happy man. After all his exploits, struggles, sins, and adventure, he is now quite settled and at peace with his universe, with himself. Though he says, "I am a nominal Catholic...", at the very core of that genius is his God who understands him, who loves him, who does not condemn him but blesses his good works and forgives his faults and grave sins. Just like everyone else, he erred and he errs, and may continue to falter but the beauty of his life is, it does not give up on what is true. So he loves Fact, Facts, and more Facts. Isn't it that the Holy Bible is the most scientific book of all times because it contains no error at all? Don't they admonish that it's much better or more correct to say that the faithful believe in the Holy Scripture because it is true?

Indeed, the scientist, the rationalist, the economist, the

mathematician, the philosopher, the poet, and the educator in Sir Ed are all but the Father's perfection of His creation, the fulfillment of His divine will for didn't the Father give man the power and authority, the stewardship and dominion over all His creation? Sir Ed, at seventy-three, continues to argue with many of the world's best minds, refuting their scientific claims, reviewing their evidence, revealing their falsehoods and fallacies, exposing their distortions and crimes, exhorting for science, the arts, law and governance, economics and education, research and technology to march forward the ages to save on cost and enjoy the benefits. He can be a very impatient man over falsity, over deception, over lies and corruption but he is adamant to mentor the confused, a responsible yet gentle shepherd to his herd, and of course, a sexy mind to the bored, usually bored, and always bored. Especially to the single-blessed, the widows, and the widowers, oh, perhaps he humors too the religious?

"*Aguray ka ah!*" He reminds me to listen well to the details of his childhood [as my naughty neuron makes a side comment to pass forward to high school because he starts his narrative, saying, "Nothing special..."]. I quickly hush the mischief as his tone is serious, very much like my strict father's, who, when we were growing up, would not allow inattention, sloth, haphazard work, no direction, no focus, not much sense. Sir Ed is quite particular with details. He wants facts as they are [a true empiricist!]. From there, he creates and transforms himself, his world, our universe.

"You can take your sweet convenient time!" He texts me one evening as I inform him I was halfway done with his biography or memoir. Oh, his precise words though in the locutionary of a euphemism made me wash the dishes with my embarrassed apron in no time, attend to my sick Kitty with less chit chat with, and purring from my legendary cat [Believe me, she was a regal queen ages ago as she listens to my woes with so much compassion, and yet in grace!], clean the rest of the equally special zoo with better gloves and mop, remind my son, JP, to brush his teeth, especially his molar and get rid of that unwanted tartar, and pour another teaspoon of black coffee [Thanks Arnold and Loida Dablo!], then gulp the fresh milk Victor and Diana Dela Cruz thoughtfully bring me and JP before midnight, to get my few neurons and little pen working all night long, all day long, all week long, until the long hours send me longing and craving for more sexy thoughts so I could write of the science and the universe of the genius with the Guinness world record longest preface [1997] in relative terms, another spectacular record making longest preface in absolute terms [2009], even beating George Bernard Shaw's preface for his "Saint Joan" written in just one longggg sentence (62,705 words), making it the THIRD LONGEST ENGLISH SENTENCE in the entire human history of print and thought, and maybe, perhaps maybe, some other hidden yet to be discovered long, longer, longest of Eduardo Rezonable Alicias Jr., the Filipino mad genius [He's a real polymath!], shining brightly side by side the heavenly bodies, with his world-famous perfection of intellectual and creative notoriety, "ERIMAKO'S PEN." [Please take pleasure with it in the Appendices!].

For just a second of sleep, he penetrates into my frequency, and sends me another text: "Emely, I email to you this Chapter 7: my arguments versus professors of Ohio State University, Brown University, John Hopkins University."

I ran to the Holy Feet, sprayed His favorite purple cologne, and whispered: "Please, I beg you! Have mercy on me! Tell this man, oh Lord, I'm not a scientist nor Marie Curie, neither Einstein's mistress! Please remind him I'm his memoirist, and I'm writing his biography, not a dissertation on the Relativity Theory! Amen."

Jesus looked down lovingly upon me and whispered: "If you don't work, you don't eat."[Thessalonians]

Oh, I forgot that Jesus, the greatest scientist, worked six days to create the universe, and rested on the seventh. That was just a Wednesday! So, I had to forego a second of sleep. The screen of my laptop was blinking. The face of the Filipino genius was beaming. My Science lesson: Get your facts right before you complain to God! Now I know why the sexy mind loves FACT, FACTS, AND MORE FACTS [though the prosody becomes problematic to yummy MEKENI! as it would be like the prohibited firecrackers, or the fuss on the gun ban! And oh, I wonder if my brother, MANONG ELREY, makes it to that Vice-Mayor's seat, with all his damsels in fervent prayers, and that he'd give me back my shotgun, forfeited in the sudden glare of the sun. Sir Ed maybe can write a pleading on my behalf, to summon Virgil's Charon and explain why the ire of Hades on my late husband's fine prostate.

THE GLORY OF HIS SCIENCE,
THE GLORY OF HIS GOD!

I whisper to Kitty, whose old purple cage is beside my lowly writing table: "Don't worry Kitty. I'm working much harder this one month to get you your prosthetic leg. The Father Genius and His son genius collaborate for this noble purpose: to extend your life so mine also will be more numbered but in years, and thus JP will have a more secured, meaningful, and joyful existence in this planet, also of apes [Darwin was an ape? Such brilliance!] but more so, of human beings, who, from creation, have been given light and life to serve one another, to be a blessing to each one, and proclaim God's Word of Salvation in good works, in good deeds. Even in humor, even through Sir Ed's humor.

Indeed, true science is the way of the faithful.
Alicias, Jr., E. is a child of God.
He has every chance to be canonized!

"A MAN SHALL NOT BE ESTABLISHED BY
WICKEDNESS: BUT THE ROOT OF THE
RIGHTEOUS SHALL NOT BE MOVED."[PSALM12:3]

PART FIVE
BEAUTIFUL LIFE OUT
OF A SEXY MIND

The Sanctification Of A Genius

"The hoary head is a crown of glory,
If it be found in the way of righteousness."
[Proverbs 16:31]

"What is your complete name?" Sir Ed surprises the shy waiter as he makes his pick of the menu. I laugh while my child looks obviously amused with the startled young man mumbling faintly a name. Though Shakespeare graces the occasion, I offer enlightenment to the rattled youth whose crowning glory is as noticeably dishevelled as his brain, totally unprepared for the Socratic interlude. His working hands, however, continue to work.

"Oh, you're Ali! Sir's last name is Alicias!"

The smile on the now radiant face of earlier weariness reveals the lad's flattery and delight for just one look at the man seated across mine and my son's leaves one not a doubt of his fine mind. But the lad now takes by mistake my little book, lying quietly on the neat table with already two big plates of Max's Combo Meal. Well, a growing boy like my JP just can't wait to nibble and devour. Food, really has to be more than punctilious for all those hormones and hungry cells.

"Ah, that's not the menu, dear! It's my little print treasure… my humble, lowly imprint to humanity though I am but the shadow of that little sister who wrote it with her tears upon the untimely death of her beloved older sister, MANANG ERLEEN." My words console the now more rattled Ali, the waiter of the hour. It's Sir Ed's turn to laugh. My epiphany seems too early. He gives me the knowledge of the ages, and the wisdom of those who care to pause, and remove the lice in their pets when summer comes. Good also to take a bath together with the canine to save on water and prevent the catastrophic drought brought by the El Nino phenomenon. Sir Ed signs his two books with enviable precision, capped with warm thoughtful benevolence, while I murmur my Ode to the West Wind. JP sighs out of little shame for his now widowed mother in faded denims and cute little black feminine blouse [courtesy of sweet Bitwin "Star" Ayalin]. Perhaps, my twelve year old is wondering why we came to a book exchange but his mother doesn't seem to mind; she's overly watchful of the tiny print lest Ali comes back and mistakes it again for some scrap.

"Well, Sir, my apologies but I can only show you my little print. This is my only copy of my own book. My former PhD advisee shipped it for me from the land of milk and honey. Oh, Sir, it's embarrassing, but I can't even afford a copy and order at Amazon.com. Sir Ed takes the little book, and scans it with his illustrious mind. I get nervous yet hope that he finds something of a cent's worth.

So, this is the book! The genius makes both a declarative and a heuristic with a nice smile on his bearded lips. MY smooth purple underneath fidgets with its velvet as I wait for more locutionary, expecting for a little compliment from the exceptionally erudite mind. However, the pink salmon lands on the table before my professor says anything interesting. My feet decide to relax on my not so new purple shoes as the much older pair had been torn out of my life's greatest pain and regret in 2017.

In between bites and mouthfuls of the Max's plate, I try to study the face of my great professor whose lectures in education and national development as well as in economics of education when I was too young, naïve, and twenty left me wondering for about three decades why eggplants in China are gigantic, when eggplants in the Philippines are but usually medium-sized, and in Ilocos, they usually come in midgets though lusciously stocky, perfect for the local stew, pinakbet, and the favorite breakfast, *poki-poki* or grilled eggplant with tomatoes, onions, eggs [eggplant omelette], and fish sauce [my late husband's favorite!]. And well, the more essential mystery, how economics, inflation, and dehumanization in education correlate or covariate with eggplants and their spectacular sizes, texture, firmness, and color. I think Regression Analysis can explain for the correlation, but up to this time of writing my professor's biography, my few neurons if they do exist, just cannot yet comprehend the esoteric framework or paradigm. Oh, I start though to get sentimental as I notice the years on his frame and on his mane but I relax again as I hear of the effervescent, exquisite brain and see the even much greater luster in that pair of magnificent emperor's eyes. With a little science in my head, I come up with several conclusions but the most weighty is, the sexy mind just cannot be outlived, archived, mediocre*d*.

While Sir Ed eats his blushing salmon like a true sage, deboning the lucky fish in the movements, precision, and dexterity of an unbeatable maestro, he shares with me and my child his reverend estate in the frames and portraits of bliss, content, and serenity. Listening to him talk of his current state of life, I remember Exodus 33:14,"...my presence shall go with thee, and I will give thee rest."

The many years of his toils and struggles have paid off, more than rewarded his sufferings and hard work.

In semi-retirement from the classroom, Sir Ed now lives in a comfortable house in Cainta Greenpark Village, Cainta, Rizal, where he serves as one member of its Board of Directors, actually for five years already. He takes a daily one-hour brisk walk in its park or rides his bike in the late afternoons, oftentimes repeatedly circling this familiar warmth when beautiful daughters of Eve are around to trim down an already graceful body. My professor puts on a naughty smile as he tells me how the female anatomy resuscitates him to life, and how it gives vigor to his knees and beard. Oh, his humor never fails to stun the mundane and the virtue yet this is a rare gift many fail to appreciate as it does rub off on sensibilities and sensitivities which only he or she who takes it as a grain of salt with an Aristotle, Tolstoy, Dickinson, Woolf, Hemingway, or even a Paul of Tarsus, Ignatius of Loyola, Thomas Aquinas, or the holy four scribes of the New Testament would be able to understand that the joke is a poker face of life: the naked truth, no matter how it may appear objectionable or bizarre. It is a redundancy to say, "I am the way, the truth, and the life." Jesus actually loved to humor as he taught of His Father's Kingdom, but the Pharisees made his jokes stale, blasphemous, and sinful; thus crucifying the greatest teacher that ever walked the face of the Earth.

"UNDERSTANDING IS A WELLSPRING OF LIFE UNTO HIM THAT HATH IT: BUT THE INSTRUCTION OF FOOLS IS FOLLY"[PROVERBS 16:22].

As the MAESTRO continues to enjoy the sea with his fine gustatory, he engages my dumb but eager little ears to more critical listening as more and more pendulums swing here and there overwhelming my pathetic brain with all those queer yet brilliant revolutionary paradigms as well as, dear Jesus, anatomies of international and local relations [economic, cultural, physiological, and oh, sexual!]. All these come and cascade like Pagsanjan Falls in his glib and gab, while distant tables seem to be getting interested now with the company of three heads: a handsome gray head, a growing head, and a swirling head. They must be envious of our more delectable menu.

Sir Ed fills me and makes me so full of his brilliant satires, metaphors, and all possible figures of speech for his genius is titillating, explosive, ballistic that I secretly gestate in euphoria, either out of sheer admiration or out of my manic passionate confusion. Oh, my subtleties make my child conspire with my pretense to fully understand and delight of the exquisite buffet of knowledge generously made free for my privileged ears and my son's. How my professor satirizes human anatomy, overpopulation in Third World economies, GNP, and per capita happiness in a continuous flux of interacting variables, and how such relationships can be altered, challenged, and repaired just sends me to interjectionary superlatives of *ohhhs, ahhs*, wows! My suprasegmentals are definitely cohabiting with my vowels, consonants, and dipthongs as I listen more and more to the genius, preoccupied pleasurably with the fish and the thought.

Reading later his research on the benefits of legalizing prostitution and reducing criminality helps me acculturate to the lingo and economics of his radical purview, but that is not to say that Sir Ed's unorthodox cognizance is bereft of even an iota or bit of moral rectitude for in fact, he is more than moral and decent when he extrapolates and theorizes that prostitutes are our equals too in a human capital of production and consumption. Oh, the University of London British Council Fellow is even more charming than Churchill, an undeniable romantic though just a little more sensory and sensual in his creative stylistics than Shakespeare's universals of the lark and the nightingale as Romeo starts to leave the bedroom of forbidden love with Juliet wanting more, desiring more of stolen hours and passionate kisses more than the two birds. It just so happens that my teacher sees not just two anatomies of the human male and the human female: not just two more, the male bird's and the female bird's; but also the anatomy of the outer space and the heavenly bodies with his 1-tailed and 2-tailed whereby the former yields a microscopic anisotropy of an irregular galaxy; the latter, a macroscopic isotropy of a spiral galaxy. Further on, he likewise hails Taal Volcano's naked core; and it's, oh, big, wide, open--with his superb math to compute and calculate the rhythm and rhapsodies of leash and unleash, of tremor and of rapture, of mount and of eruption, well, explosion. The Big Bang comes later in our interdiscourse of transdisciplinary CDA or critical discourse analysis while our finger food wait patiently to be nibbled in the now higher temperature of a room full of bored yet hungry, famished carnivores and herbivores.

"FOR HE SATISFIETH THE LONGING SOUL AND FILLETH THE HUNGRY SOUL WITH GOODNESS"[PSALM 107:9].

With the fortunate gracious fish almost a delightful memory, Sir Ed continues to lead me into the wellsprings of knowledge and the wisdom that emanates from all these gems, whether sapphire or ruby, gold or silver, truth or falsity, probability or nonprobability or impossibility, skewness or skewer, erect or rambunctious, arid or succulent. His favorite, statistics is as fascinatingly intrepid though at the onset, quite petulant to my below average computational skills but which the late Dr. Umila rewarded with a 1.0, equivalent to an "A" in my Advance Research and Statistics PhD class in UP, mistaking my heuristic gambit as a genius of numbers. Oh, my brilliant fatherly professor (Dr. Umila) who earned his PhD in the United States of America must have appreciated more the poetry of my nonsense. Anyway, the salmon-eating genius before me begins to talk of his most significant revolutionary contribution to education research and evaluation, his Variance Partitioning Analysis [VPA] Model. Gosh, I murmured in my swirling nervous head that there was no need for a tete-a-tete on that Regression Analysis breakthrough as basis to determine who, among the teachers teaches the most, the average, and teaches the least, or perhaps, teaches nothing at all. The genius of this novel teacher performance evaluation paradigm with now some artifacts and archeology of the quintessential salmon on his fingers and upper lip, drives me deep into the radical brilliance of his **VPA** brainchild, which in my limited capacity to understand, directly, proportionally correlates student achievement to an excellent or effective teacher. Well, Sir Ed does not like much the input-oriented, teacher-centered framework of evaluating the teacher as far as merit of performance is concerned. He has always loved anything round, succulent, or luscious yet fluffy. So, his **VPA** Model comes in a pie that "represents the total variance of a set of achievement scores on a particular criterion." Here, he favors an output-oriented and student-centered framework of teacher effectiveness evaluation. His pie, of course is more than delectable to the education research erudite as it is "partitioned into various angular portions representing the effects attributable to the set of teacher factors." Jesus, I whisper this time to my child to behave as his good manners and right conduct are directly attributable to his rather anti-social, quite volatile widowed mother. But, of course, I continue to pretend before my exceptionally gifted professor that my four and only four neurons are absorbing and processing his pie of many equations [How I wish we just go to SHAKEY'S or PIZZA HUT than talk of the statistical pie! But those interested to get a scientific discussion of the **VPA** Model, just check the Appendices. My task is more to tell the tales of his life than his statistical tails of 1-tailed and 2-tailed. Heavens!!

Oh no! Sir Ed intercepts and aborts my modus to abandon ship. He asks, "Emely, do you get it?"

My old professor, though even more attractively handsome in years, must be really a man of greater virtue now for he must be patiently and prudently assuming that my little brain is of multiple intelligences just like his. So I go, "Ah Sir, I believe your VPA is very sound, very scientific, more than objective and brilliantly principled [as if I knew and understood!]. But how about controlling for extraneous variables [Here come the villains!], say, students get lower scores from quizzes because they love K-pop or K-soap?" My God, the Regression Analysis expert falls into momentary silence of a half nanosecond but then he recovers fast though I somewhat miss the representational register [Oh, planned and deliberate discourse strategy to shift topic or change gears!]. I jump at the opportune to nominate another topic [yes! should be mutually intelligible! not lopsided! oh, excuses for the feeble intellect!] as nearby tables are really getting and getting more envious of our interdiscourse, but which only my professor gets the subliminal pleasure while I freeze and get frigid with endless, infinite variables.

"What other hobbies or extra-curricular activities do you engage in, Sir, aside from brisk walking, that is your physics, and girl watching, that is both your biology and chemistry?" I sigh in relief as the erudite head gets into a little astronomical motion within the trite ordinariness of my orbit. Sir Ed smiles with the undefiant heart of blissful existence, the good life.

My professor now starts to speak in the lyric and idyll of contentment, of success, of security, of a solid home, of genuine faith, and of inexhaustible dreams and unabated hope. While now I listen to a thankful man for the blessings that have come forth out of his relentless pursuits and struggles. I remember the sad eyes and the pain in them as he earlier talked of the history of his pioneering extraordinary education research, the **VPA** MODEL. The past seems to still haunt the former UP professor as he spoke of the lameduck and the lackluster of an input-oriented or teacher-centered framework for teacher evaluation. Though his words were passionate for a scientific evaluation and computation of merit over the subjective culture of public relations, affiliations, and affinities, his eyes gave his heart away. I felt the depth of his pain as I saw momentarily, in my old memory, a devastating episode of pride and prejudice; of a gang of masquerading intellectuals who robbed, abused, and wasted such a rare genius for the frivolities and fringe benefits of their deliberate oversight or their unthinking stupid of their dismal beings. "Hush, hush, hush." My more saintly neuron murmurs.

Yet, the illustrious one did not lose the light; amidst dejection, he kept going. Many thought he did not have a God. He proved them all wrong.

A WISE SON MAKETH A GLAD FATHER. [PROVERBS 15:20}

Torrents came but "The Oustanding Ilocano Educator" has always been faithful to the Father. He refused to be beaten by mediocrity, treachery, and selfishness. His humor helped him keep his faith, to chart his destiny, and so now, we are deeper into our interdiscourse yet at this point, a little more laidback but quite delightfully sentimental, domesticated, settled. The sexiness though is always apparent; no, blatantly obscene, but refreshingly truthful.

From time to time, Sir Ed goes home to a well-deserved property at the very heart of one of the TEN GREAT CITIES IN THE WORLD, what used to be CIUDAD FERNANDINA during the Spanish Colonization in the country's history. Vigan is the real heritage and home of the archetypal subconscious yet non-archetypal genius, and in here, his renaissance abode sits well amidst the paradoxical conclave of urban and rural, as the reincarnated great Northern city now beams of the hustle and bustle of modern living while it has the romantic fragments of classic simple existence.

Sir Ed's lordship of the ERIMAKO'S FARM traces its beginnings in the land of King Arthur and his Round Table [Ours at Max's is rectangular!]. What used to be Engleland, Englaland of the Angles, the Jutes, and the Saxons though in time, it was just the Angles and the Saxons, never mind the Jutes [maybe they got marooned too in some Lotus Island!]. His search for the "Holy Grail" of knowledge in that great land saw him fall into the woeful abyss of sin as he lingered and dwelt in those islands of the intoxicating Homerian Lotus, oh but much more of the tempting wildness of mystic cherry blossoms, perhaps transplanted for the seduction of an unlikely saint; a genius and a saint but who'd never bother to fret of the difference as his Regression Analysis would always put these both as covariates in the same framework. ERIMAKO thus meets KeeKee at the United Kingdom in this leg [Oh, not my Kitty's lifeless leg!] of a man's journey to sin, redemption, and GREATNESS. The search for more light in science, conscience in education, and the integrity of reason and philosophy at this point in time, gets temporarily muddled with mortal sin [Remember biblical King Solomon?], for THE FLESH IS WEAK THOUGH THE HEAD IS HUGE.

But, who among us [of flesh, bones, and blood], does not falter? Even Popper with his "falsification principle" falsifies himself. Hume is as lost as himself either, while Eistein keeps turning in his grave [I suppose] for the outcomes [Thanks Sir Ed's VPA!] of his Theory of Relativity for all the nukes, above, around, and underneath this planet, with Nagasaki and Hiroshima as the first ill-fated sites of the cosmic brilliance and evil of a man. The Law of Balance weighs more for the physics and chemistry of human greed, despotism, and bestiality; while the good in human nature continuously gets exploited, corrupted, debased. But, there is the TRUE LIGHT that protects the CHAMPIONS OF RADIANT LIGHT. Sir Ed has been delivered by the True Light from the nadirs of darkness; Hades was made to pay more woefully and damningly, and Charon had to put him back on that boat to the shores of the RED SEA. The True Light sought for its champion from the dungeons of wretchedness that bewitched and beguiled him for the hours and years of human folly and utter frailty. The True Light sent its army of angels to search for the fallen MAESTRO ERIMAKO.

AND THEY FOUND HIM. "They compassed me about; yea, they compassed me about: but IN THE NAME OF THE LORD, I will destroy them."[Psalm 118:11]. Sir Ed climbed his way out of the wretched bowels of sin, of evil and the devil, with the help of people who truly care and love him—his family, friends, and students, they, who are his good army of angels on Earth that he may fulfil his mission as a Champion of Light. God the Father has, since time immemorial, overlooked the sins of His chosen ones, His disciples, His apostles, His saints, His priests and deacons, His holy women, His favoured men and gave them armies of angels to help them through the temptations of Satan. As I was writing, drafting, revising, especially the encoding, and printing of Sir Ed's biography, THE DEVIL, HIMSELF CAME TO BEGUILE, TEMPT, AND STOP ME. But the ALMIGHTY FATHER sent me His army of good angels [FR. Ubaldous Djonda, an Indonesian SVD priest—to buy me the Microsoft Office and technical help, patiently and diligently assisting me and JP[in his blue accented logo], especially, the spiritual and moral strength, together with Fr. Roy Matthew, an Indian priest who fed me and my son, right at the ST. JOSEPH'S SHRINE and who'd pray for my guidance and perseverance, and ask me regularly the progress of my book, as well as giving widow and now, fatherless child their provisions; FR. Leonard Rosario Shankar [Bangladeshi priest], for the mantle he sent for me, all the way from Bangladesh for the brown table mantle but miraculously, with finely embroidered BLUE FlOWERS, resembling those of the BLESSED MOTHER'S [of my childhood that I shall recount in full on my next little book!], Fr. Thaddeus [Bangladeshi priest], who patiently met with me in UST [as he got lost in the campus!] to hand me the mantle, at the middle of my despair on whether to just cry and give up, doubting my capacity of mind, energy, time and resources to finish the book, and the good young priest, came in his dark blue deacon's clothes; Sr. Mary Celine Santos, SPC, who'd send me almost everyday bible and inspirational words, with her incessant, unfailing prayers, love, and support for me and my child; so were my dear old closest friends, Jayne Velasco-Blanco, a UP Diliman Math Major graduate [frequently waking me up with the Gospel of the day, by text message all the way from Canada, or through online inspiration, with Canadian missionary priest, Fr. Luciano's heartfelt homiletics!], and Nerisse Bundoc-Dizon, another UP-Diliman Math Major graduate and Math teacher, reminding me to take intervals of rest, all the way as well from the United States of America!; Dr. Josefa "Fe" Nava, a retired UP–Diliman Research and Statistics professor [who specialized in statistics in the U.S., reminding me to pray, reflect, and discern for God's message to me; the young "new" Sr. Tine Bajarin, expressing her support and love for me and JP, a batallion of Christian Pastors and women, bringing daily to my ears, heart, and mind God's words [through Radio DZAS, including my *tsinoy* former UST Graduate student, James, and his Chinese mom for gifting me the radio, and Kring Fontejon, former principal of JP, for the Bible verses in Filipino]; the Jesuit priests who continue to pray for me and my family, including the guest Jesuit priest on a

Sunday evening mass at the Church of the Holy Sacrifice, who inspired and imprinted into my soul the GRACE OF THE TRUE LIGHT, helping me to focus my writing on its theme, and not fall into pornography or the sin of flesh as the DEVIL TEASED, ENTICED, AND SEDUCED ME NO END while writing especially PART THREE of the biography that it took me about two weeks to draft and re-draft, to revise and revise it; my ROOSEVELT COLLEGE family, especially, my graduate students who'd come to our home, and give us food even late at night or early morning, with their good handsome husbands, or right there in my classroom, with Bitwin "Star" Ayalin, dressing me up, boasting my sagging morale, a true STAR in the midst of darkness, of course, the providential gifting me of the beautiful holy rosary of the Blessed Mother by thoughtful and loving Diana Dela Cruz, accompanied so graciously by her handsome Victor; all the Good Samaritans, acquaintances and total strangers, who'd help me and my child, in one way or the other, cope with the stress while I was writing, encoding, and printing the book, like the compassionate and warm, SARI SARI STORE owner, Flor, who'd chit chat with me of my burdens, the kind tricycle driver who quickly came to our aid when our vehicle's front tire just totally deflated, and Mang Jun who fixed it patiently, warmly, and well so I could bring JP to STARLAND INTERNATIONAL SCHOOL, with the ever patient school principal, Sir Jay, and Teacher Ezel, bearing with my volatility and arrogance at a time that my son did nasty in the class, but I was just too exhausted and sleepless from encoding the biography, my tolerance was even much much lower, I ranted before them; of course, my family, my dear father, PAPANG ELOY, encouraging, urging, supporting me to persevere and not give up on the book especially with all the technical brouhahas, praying the NOVENA TO OUR BLESSED MOTHER, OUR PERPETUAL HELP AND SUCCOR, with our nice and kind stepmother, Tita Chelie; my sisters Ely and Estela Marie for watching over our house and the tomb of my husband in Ilocos, that I'd not fret too much and so, I could focus on my writing, including, of course, my niece, Laarni Guce-Arranz, who'd pay for our Ilocos bills despite her hectic schedule as bank teller in BANCO DE ORO, as well as Manong Rey, Manang Baby Lou, and Errol Anthony who put down my blood pressure with their own medicines [as the medical malpractice, killing my husband pains me so much, I do not like going anymore to hospitals and to see doctors at this juncture of my vulnerable existence!], my youngest sister, Ethel Consuelo, for her sweet photos with her family on FACEBOOK, lifting me back to those clouds and skies of joy and bliss when my home was still perfectly sublime in this planet]; my twelve year-old son, JOSEPH MARY PETER PAUL LAMB[LORENZO ANSELMO MARY THE BLESSED or JP, helping me with my depression, my eccentricity in my lowly writing [Top Secret!], and the errands of buying cans of sardines for our pets, and our meals of pork barbecue and the pig's ears [for me to hear better God's whispers as I wrote!], of course, THE MAN, himself whose life I've been BATTLING WITH SATAN, to chronicle and write! The MAESTRO'S impressive PATIENCE with his student's burdens, faults, and shortcomings even her [Emely] rogue, verbal inanity and shameful onanism, telekinetic pornography, toxic fury, and philosophical vehemence as well as her worst, her suicidal taunts, cruising into nihilism and Nietsche's vapid, engaging him in the crossfires of lust and faith, of arrogance and humility, of squalor and greatness, of life and death!; BUT THE MIRACLE OF IT ALL, our little zoo, EMELY'S MENAGERIE [Thanks Sir Ed!], which just noisily, silently, peacefully, and mysteriously kept me SANE in the long hours of my DEEP PAIN, missing the ONE AND ONLY ONE MAN I will always always love, my LORENZ. Had they not comforted me, had they not chatted and listened to me, had they not danced, sang, and prayed with me, had they not borne and understood my wrath, my cursing, my violence in mind and blood, I could have lost my own LIGHT in the vicissitudes of human filth, vulnerability, despair, misery, ugliness, and hopelessness. But, they came, they stayed, they watched, they barked, and purred for me to realize the SANCTITY OF LIFE AND THE SACRILEGE OF SUICIDE. The FATHER sent me too His formidable squadron and fleets of good angels in different forms and faces so I, myself could battle my own evils, TO TRIUMPH over the temptations and forces of the eternally damned, and fulfil my own life's purpose, my mission to the world I never thought I had. And my life saver in the vastness of despair? AUTHORHOUSE, UNITED STATES! I could not believe then that the rough waters and high seas would get into a beautiful calm: AUTHORHOUSE agreed to print and publish me again, but this time, with my name not hidden. "Christ is risen; He appears to Mary Magdalene, then to others. He sends the apostles to preach, promises that signs shall follow faith---He ascends into heaven" [Mark 16].

ERIMAKO'S PEN! The pivotal point of redemption, of resurrection of a fallen King. This internationally acclaimed poem hailed and put the forgotten, abandoned, dejected King to his rightful kingdom: THE TOP OF THE WORLD. ERIMAKO, the author, the poet, and the nom de plume ROSE TO GREATNESS, after the gruelling wanderings and misery in desolate lands, raging waters, and woeful bowels of darkness. The MAESTRO penned the world famous, "Humor and Madness"[1997], and its sequel, "Humor and Madness, Jr."[2009], earning him a GUINNESS WORLD RECORD recognition for the former. These accolades and achievements proceeded from mortal sin to salvation. The GOOD in the man, in the genius HAS WON OVER EVIL: "Blessed is the man who perseveres with life's trials for he shall reap the crown of life."

FOR LIFE HAS ALL ITS GEMS AND ITS OWN MISGIVINGS! And, it goes in circular orbits and patterns.

Well, SALVACION. Of real time.

The almost obscene yet perfect Salvacion in faithful representation of human instinct and passion is the unmistaken, forgivable QUEEN INAMORATA of Lord Erimako. She is the magnificent perfection of beauty upon the eyes of her beholder. Sir Ed claims to plant all the organics in the farm where his queen dwells for indeed, the body is sacred; ERIMAKO AND SALVACION ARE ONE, and so, another magnum opus, "EJACULATES FROM THE HEART", that when Sir Ed handed me the copy of such an *obra* on love and romance, between a genius septuagenarian and a true phantom of youthful beauty, I fell into the nothingness of my being, the nude perfection of a human HEART, beating, yes beating to give the dead of a thousand times [Shakespeare], their hopes and their lives. I cannot write more of Salvacion as I made a promise to my professor to keep my pen off the grass, oh, the rose garden, the lovely farm where lovely Salvacion also dwells. However, I am likewise spilling some of the beans! In one of our online repartees and more interdiscourses, I got ERIMAKO in a no-holds- barred discourse mode [Thanks for my little DA!], and here's the genius's stream of consciousness [Praise ye, uncle Freud!] that I pillaged while I fried another chicken thigh and breast for my growing son's hormones:

"Oh Salvacion! She is one awesome mystery in my life thus far! Is she real or simply fictional? That I don't know as yet. But she has dominated, over two and one half years, my consciousness, my dreams and fantasies…regardless of who are what she is in real life! But hell, so what? Real or unreal, so emphatically both psychological and nomological. Is she the will-o-the wisp, the ignis fatuus that leads me to rarefied and/or even mindboggling heights of destiny? Who knows? I don't know, but again, I say: never mind and no matter, real or surreal, Salvacion is defining a significant portion of my sunset years! For now, I recall the song of my youth: *que sera sera*, whatever will be will be! I have one eschatological question though: for what purpose or meaning did she ever come into my consciousness? Why? For what reason, purpose? Why doesn't she fade away, sublimate into the rarefaction of ethereality, surreality?"

Dear Jesus, I burned the chicken leg and breast! My late husband, dancing sexy and oh, so gracefully just like old times flashed not in the pan but in my seduced mind. And we danced, twirled, danced, until we made love, while our canine and feline looked away from the sacrilege of a living wife and her dead husband. Linda, our dog howled and our cats whissed and gnashed their teeth, with our rabbit's hole shaking in the horrors of lost love. Then the radio opened by itself, with the Christian Pastor exhorting, "Bring your thoughts back on God!" And, I ran to the MAN ON THE CROSS, and wept for my mortal sin.

Romance at 73! Clandestine or not, truth or illusion, it is the Island of Serenity and Joy for the MAESTRO, Lord of ERIMAKO'S FARM, unexpected paradise, right at the bosom of immortalized Fernandina. A wise man indeed pleases the Father.

The MAESTRO speaks fondly of his twin tropical cottages like his twin grand-daughters, sweet, pretty, and smart **Ima** and **Leona** who excel in academics, well, no longer surprising having such superior genes of the entire family tree, with the genius as their grandparent prototype. Each cottage is complete with the amenities of convenient comfortable living, perfect for respite from the chaos of the universe. There is a function hall, well, kind of expected in Lord Erimako's Farm. How can the world stay away from such magnetic force, from such sphere and orbit? Only the cave man would.

"There's a swimming pool in my farm, if you love to swim." Sir Ed tells me. My heart flutters as I remember learning the breast stroke right there, in the huge swimming pool of the University of the Philippines, Diliman, enjoying by myself the pool of the country's top intellectual shenanigans, with the able and fatherly guidance of Mang Ped, my late husband's good friend in all those thirty-seven years that he dedicated his service and life in the university. But my fun, happy recollection is cut abruptly when the MAESTRO blurts, "Everyone is welcome but women should swim in my pool only when they wear 2-piece bikini!" My jaw drops upon my elegy. He turns to my son, and say: "You too should wear 2-piece when you come swim in my pool!" JP laughs as he knows by now how his mother's professor loves to joke.

I know I can never bask in the greatness of the man's pool, as only legendary muses and sirens could eternally sing and frolic in the waters of perfection. This pool's owner, the man who taught me when I was too shy, daydreaming, and twenty of the various forms of promiscuity: the promiscuity of ignorance and mediocrity, the promiscuity of indifference or lethargy, the promiscuity of miseducation or its dereliction, the promiscuity of the tyranny of deception, betrayal, and lies, and the promiscuity of power play, and its cohabiting concubinage with evil.

The 2-piece swimwear does not only intimidate and agitate my now physiological state, but agitates as well the metaphors of my not so distant memory. The widow has no right to splash her body on the blood of saint. Yes, her next book, "The Blood Of Saint" [Orillos 2019, in the works] is now almost baking the pages on her wee hours of woeful tears.

I continue to listen to Sir Ed as he makes and takes a left and right turn of his current indulgences and proclivities while

I silently cry my tears inside my heart. But, of course, the mood does not last long as the author of a GWRs is never, never a dull boy. In seconds, I hear myself laughing and talking in the delightful madness of such a sexy afternoon. The genius takes me into an exhilarating roller coaster of talk and rhetoric on all of life's many faces or vicissitudes: sentiments, struggles, adventures, victories, betrayals, mortal sins, frustrations, secrets, disillusionment, angst, and of course, humor, cerebral and well, more than prurient. Yet again, the privilege of intimating my dismal four neurons [with hopefully, an emerging fifth!] with the Filipino demigod, the Philippines' Einstein [Could there be another polymath farming or fishing in any of the seven thousand plus islands of the entire archipelago? or, maybe still in his or her mother's womb!] is worth all my sighs and yawns for sweet elusive sleep for almost two years now since April 11, 2017. Glad that my cold *Gulaman at Sago* drink is still half full, hence the vestiges of ire get into another shelf of my memory; and oh yes, the sexy mind never fails to satiate all kinds of appetites, in fact, every interdiscourse with him leaves one craving for more, desiring the bottomless.

But, as Sir Ed tells me that he does not anymore drive longer than three hours, and that he does not go farther than necessary, really just enjoying physics in moderation though he is quick to add that he prefers chemistry and biology in the park, my heart once more turns into smithereens with the memories of my husband, sitting beside me, and patiently like a saint, clasping his Novena to Our Mother of Perpetual Help, with his rosary, as I drove crazier than Mad Max whenever we were late in fetching JP from school, our one and only child. I try to focus my heart and soul on the words of my professor whose largeness is just too much for the head I carry on my shoulders, with all the flagellation and heavy crosses. Oh, it seems like only the Saturday before today that I sat with my mediocrity, fantasies, and oh, decrepit in his classes, with me walking down the stairs of the UP College of Education carrying tons of books plus all the eggplants and the magician's crystal balls in my poor head, trying to reconcile sex education with human empowerment, institutional identity, educational leadership, economic stability, and moral ascendancy. And while walking myself and my good friend, Paul, to the Oblation for some epiphany and more air, we'd exploit each other's minds and imagination of Plato's classic educational system [Was he really elitist?], the socialists [Oh, not too safe, perhaps!], and the progressivists [Welcome to 21st century!], as all kinds of balls would pop, bounce, and toss somewhere in our schematic diagrams that were mostly representational-phatic than visual-transactional. How I and my mestizo classmate [He'd usually tell me then how my thoughts flirted with his identity crisis!] loved to discuss and laugh of our lessons of torrid rebirth and vociferous reawakening to intellectual bliss and moral freedom. The youngest as I was in Sir Ed's intensely liberating and truly hot classes, I could only scribble, Is he an immortal, punishing me for my voyeur of the moon's butt one night the owl perched on our guava tree, for doesn't the goddess Diana love to pee when the world is fast asleep, and there I was, making verses on her beautiful sparkling and glittering diamond. Hence, I'd rush to my double-deck and dream and dream of that strange world I wanted to conquer in the seasons and years of my own toils, wanderings, and hopeful prayers. I remember having cried to the endearing and great Fr. James Reuter, SJ, of my disappointments and frustrations of not being allowed to have hair rollers when climbing my favorite mango trees, way back in high school, for they were the nests of my little colourful thoughts. Ordinariness has always given me the real beauty of my existence, born, reared, raised in a barrio. And, Sir Ed's classes in UP just mesmerized me to find sophistication and elegance in my mundane. So, I had my fantasies of the genius professor and the very young, dumb, and plain student. However, fate said, "Not this one."

Sir Ed believes that law and medicine can be both furiously sick and evil for their horrendous negligence and crimes that remain institutionally constant, unchecked, and shamelessly glaring. He talks of their unbridled power as tempting good men to rape and exploit the feeble of humanity, and cracks a sarcastic joke to whiplash the wretchedness of some major law, "So, at 84, I can also rape!" Of course, the genius is just fed up and tired of the short-sightedness, or is it a euphemism to call the stupidity of limiting crime and punishment below the octogenarian? My silence is more deafening [My late husband's surgeon was 82! And I was too stupid not to know early on! Now, he's 84 and kicking filthy rich, strutting in the hallways of his limpid!] than my husband's tomb as anger once again comes to the fore of my memory like giant, raging, and ravaging waves to the seawall. But, I discipline myself to behave. My professor's emperor's eyes blink in the serious unmonotony of seconds to extol on the vigilance of the educated mind to be consistently watchful, suspicious, untrusting or distrusting of exorbitant intentions, for the good in each person, he claims is corrupted by its own irresponsibility and domicile of thought-- rather, parochialism, insularism, and indolence to pay attention, research, and question. Oh, I suddenly make an infamous yet truthful insertion to his passionate discourse and monologue on social justice and injustice. He laughs with me rather insidiously as I tell him of my own abdication and trust on the good and best of medicine for the tragedy and the trauma it has caused my sensibilities and the deep pain it inflicted in my heart as well as its corruption of my child's innocence and dreams for having taken away from us, in the sudden swing of life's pendulum our beloved Papa Lorenz. Because of the evil of medical malpractice [that does not get punished in the Philippines!], I whisper to Sir Ed that I now self-medicate as I have totally lost my trust on the good and best of that world. Sir Ed breaks into a hearty guffaw when I add that I bring down my blood pressure with the long tested medicines of my older brother, Manong Elrey, our eldest, Manang Baby Lou, and our younger brother, Errol. But the great science in his head gives me a gentle yet firm caveat to see my cardiologist and buy the digital wonder as he says very affordable and practical. Oh, my neuron of happiness jumps gleefully, realizing the genius seated across me is full of human compassion albeit the radical sophistication in his head proliferates like the mushrooms and fire trees in Ilocos Sur, after a good rain, not to forget the mirthful tadpoles and laughing frogs I used to swim with in our fish pond when I was a child; oh, such lovely things akin to my professor's penchant for the green jokes of humouring humor.

The metaphor of the 2-piece bikini now becomes a delightful course with its discourse frames marked by unexpected but pleasant presuppositions, implicatures, and entailments though it leaves a poignant bitterness in memory. Well, of course, its critical register is punctuated by the concerted synthesis of the professor and the student that the evil of medical malpractice should or must be put to a stop soonest than sooner for the much greater damage it can cause, statistically bifurcated with widows, widowers, and orphans, if it remains a status quo. My professor likewise ridicules the intellect for its failure to prepare itself, for its lack of scientific discipline, and the self for its moral servitude to absolute trust. Yes, he never minces his words when he speaks of facts and satirizes the absolute. But while he now undresses his own post modern bias, there fixed in his core his faith in God as he solemnly prays with me and my child before we even started to fill ourselves with the grace of such a beautiful sexy afternoon.

With darkness beginning to enshroud and envelop the well lit city, I remind myself not to lose the precious gems of my first ever face to face sit-down, intimate interdiscourse with my UP professor since 1984, when I wrote on my notebook, on the first day of class, "IS HE A MAD MAN? GOD, I'M JUST TOO CRAZY MYSELF TO KNOW."

Oh, Sir Ed again manifests beautifully his heart and his humanity as he thoughtfully reminds me and my child to bring home the still crispy chicken thigh and breast left on our plates. So touched, I quickly tell Ali to wrap as well whatever is left of that lucky salmon. The sage smiles as the sun sets somewhere, and I feel good of myself.

He shakes my hand, looks straight into my eyes, touches the rather growing head of my son, as he departs with, "LET'S DO IT AGAIN!"

While he begins to fade in my sight, but this time just for a week or two, unlike the thiry-five years of lost history between the brilliant professor and his dumb student, I search for some more words to describe him, aside from the evident of the here and now.

Happy. Fulfilled. Gracious and humble. INCOMPARABLE LIGHT! And I drove widow and child to their rabbit's hole with a joyful heart. Genuine happiness is contagious. My forlorn found solitude in the life of a beautiful human being. He, now, is my MONA LISA.

Second meet up. A Déjà vu! But more!

We meet again in the same restaurant, at the same time, and the familiar rectangular table near the glass entrance, and near the corner.

Max's Sta Lucia today has almost the same number of busy and buzzing tables on their respective square meters of costly space. JP follows his black and tangerine mother to the unisex or bisexual rest room, carrying with him the invaluable old laptop [but used to be burdensome when it was brand new!] that is usually now the apple of discord between the millennial and the hot mama, oh, the post- menopausal widow. Son turns his back as the mother sits on the throne. "Oh, is this one of those last mother and son bonding moments in a public toilet?" I start to feel the pangs of loneliness, of despair, and of fear. JP is growing fast, and my lad is dangerously handsome. I wonder how life would be when he gets his own family although he's been telling me, he will never leave his Mama Emely alone. But as I flush the uncomplaining toilet, my mood changes. I wash my hands with the light blue liquid soap and ready my now much shorter hair as well as my now alerted four neurons for the man who carries billions and billions of all smart neurons of which fifty per cent is the world's sexiest in the whole universe of human neurons [just wondering if clones can possibly have more than of my four neurons?].

This second Saturday of February 2019 witnesses another book-gift giving by the great professor [Maybe JP wished for pizza instead as he would often ask me, "Mama, do I have to read all your books and Papa's? Can you just share them to schools on the mountain?"] Of course, my child does not fully realize yet how those prints are priceless. There are four this time, and I feel all the more privileged. Three are fabulously out of the press, while one is more than fabulous but still in press. Perfect for my four neurons! [As of late, the fourth print is officially out in the market!].

The yellow-brown book "Evaluating Government Structures and Policies: The Factual Versus The Counterfactual [2017]." discusses and illustrates impact evaluation, i.e., young and old countries,--isms like cameralism, federalism; policy manipulable determinants, and variables, and more variables, etc. etc. etc. But I like most the Chapter 9, "The Prostitutes: Let Them Be or Not Be?" Sir Ed cites here the latest world statistic of more or less 13,828,700 flesh traders, with China on top of the list. "My gosh! Everything is really made in China!" My shy neuron quips. My professor takes it back for his signature, and his benevolent "Compliments." While Sir

Ed affixes his identity on his print gift, I fall into mortal sin as my imagination cannot stop laughing on the obscenity of the syphilis of the toe caused by the athlete's foot disease in the world record making "Humor and Madness, Jr.[2009]" of the madness of this genius before me who wears again his favorite *purontong* or knee-length walking shorts. However, my moroseness plagues me as I suddenly realize that the toe syphilis can be better and safely cured by antibiotics than the TURT or the Trans Urethral Resectioning of the Toe, that could kill the athlete who seems to be very fit for the Olympics, but caution for the antibiotics, as it might be a blood thinner! Oh, if only I knew...if only I knew...Now, I understand better why Sir Ed loves chemists and their chemistry. But I notice my professor studying me now so I mumble a quick penance, and hope that the good priests [Fr. Uz, Fr. Roy, Fr. Leonard, Fr. Bien, and Fr. George] are praying for my soul at the moment. Chapter 9 of the book hooks me into a more cerebral [again, if I have a brain!] objective, scientific, critical, and statistical analysis of the social reality. But since time immemorial, as old as the Old Testament, prostitution indeed has evolved and continues to evolve in many other forms. Most controversial is the story of Mary Magdalene, who fell into grave sin, and sinned and sinned until she wiped with her best oil, her best perfume the feet of Jesus as she wept. She is very much in heaven, and she is one of the favoured women of Jesus, the very first who witnessed His resurrection from death, His rising from the dead. My Theology in the Royal Pontifical University reminds me though not to get too far with my imagination as it is a mortal sin not to restrain and discipline it; too much leads to malice. But my UP education tells me to reason with science and facts. I'm just too glad, Sir Ed's discussion of the social malady is scientific, and that lessens my guilt, for the Christian Pastors over DZAS extol for the laity to be biblical theologians: "Know more of God by reading the Holy Scriptures. So. I resolve to read further of my professor's Chapter 9 after our second interdiscourse over crisp fried chicken and juicy breast with a special not so native chicken *con arroz caldo* [I wonder if Sir Ed earlier asked Sheira, the Persian-looking waitress, for the chicken feet.]. Oh, I wish now my professor didn't eat the foot and mouth disease. But I need to set aside for the meantime Chapter 9 to focus on other agenda though at the back of my head, I 'm just too curious to find out if my professor's facts tied up and tightened with some moral orifice so at least there is more light at the end of the tunnel. I likewise try to overcome my current affliction of so much crime in my head as the moments of deep sorrow, the long hours of excruciating pain, the non-punishment of the big hospital and its fifteen medical malpractitioners, who continue to practice their rotten medicine and comfortably escape the law for their crime of syndicated murder and conspiracy due to the indifference and neglect of Filipinos and their government to put forward a much stronger law that goes after doctors of medicine who deliberately cause the death, or kill their own patients out of their greed for money, cause my emotive/affective neuron to go berserk, plotting so much gore for the cold killers of my loving husband, like the perfect sophisticated radical philosophical and creative violence, justice, and vengeance in the films, "The Brave One" and "Silence of the Lambs." Oh, I just love Jodi Foster and I hope she will agree to film the autobiography, "The Blood Of Saint" I am now rewriting, in memory of my fallen husband, LORENZO QUIAMBAO ORILLOS, former UP-Diliman professor. While the Dante Alighieri before me blinks and squints with time, I see myself kissing the feet of the Holy Man On The Cross with my tears, and some purple cologne to delight My God, My Creator, and My Saviour, every night, since the tragic death of my beloved, this I do so as not to be overpowered by the Prince of Darkness, Lucifer. Since I was around seven or eight, it seems

I have already been bestowed the mission to write of God's Kingdom, of His Goodness and Mercy, of His Protection and Salvation though the mission is just manifesting itself to me more clearly now, and I need to battle Satan in my deepest pain in life to carry out and fulfil my mission though I am but a sinner and a sinful woman. As Sir Ed shifts his weight with the fundamentals of gravity, geometry, and felicity, I whisper my apology to St. Mary Magdalene for dragging her into the schema of history, fact, and story. I just wish I could tell my professor how Chapter 9 of his book leads me to the edges of reason, faith, and sanity. JP, my son elbows me a little as he very well knows, his mother is cohabiting with some odd thought again; nasty or not, pure or gore, it behooves me, and so I murmur, "FORGIVE ME, FATHER."

Sir Ed must have also been born a prophet and a seer as he'd always text me from this second meet up, "Emely, more power...more light!; or," Emely, more power...more inspiration!" Oh, his brilliance really comes from God though his humor is subject to more pleadings in the courts of literature and cultural studies, cognitive psychology and neurolinguistics, grammar of heresy and grammar of faith. Whatever. Whatever. Whatever. Better humouring than penalizing the toe syphilis with over taxation, or worst, performing the TURT [Trans Urethral Resectioning of the Toe], performing in haste the fatal surgery, after giving the BLOOD THINNER ANTIBIOTIC to the very much able and capable athlete to run and compete in the Olympics, then conspire with the entire hospital, corrupt investigators, and media/journalists to hide the crime, and hoard or burn the vital medical records, especially the BLOOD LOSS RECORDS of the patient they killed from the Trans Urethral Resectioning of the Toe. A CLASSIC CASE OF PERFECT MURDER. And a classic play of Shakespeare. How I wish the fate of the evildoers is as classic as Virgil's "Divine Inferno." Or, in a more revolutionary perspective, as sophisticated as Jodi Foster's "The Brave One" and "Silence of the Lambs" though my neuron in constant amuck, prefers Dr. Lecter's style. For the meantime, I console myself with the pig's ears. "Mama!" Again, JP, my son, my angel interrupts and stops my CRIMES IN MY HEAD. As we go to the Church of the Holy Sacrifice, my tears fall on the grounds my husband walked and in which he made his imprints for thirty-seven years while the priest says, "Believe in God's Promises!" And as we visit the Claretian Church in Teacher's Village for Ash Wednesday, I fall to my genuflection with so much remorse as the main theme in the Holy Altar says: "COME BACK TO ME."

The Brown Book On Fire, "Forms of Government and the Occurrence of Coups D' Etat, c2009". My God, again! Sir Ed discusses here the correlation of running a country, in what form, and plotting a coup, and he uses the statistical ANOVA or analysis of variance to get the coup means across categories, and not only that, he also identifies which government is of "lesser virtue" [more hospitable!] to coups. Jesus Christ! He is really one unbelievable mind as he researches into, controlling for the variance of extraneous variables, the connection between the forms of government and the occurrence of coups. Like Juan Linz, he theorized that the presidential form of government is more hospitable to the occurrence of coups. And, he tested his theory with the use of, among others, Multiple Regression Analysis. Wow! My UP professor just toys with government forms and coups, using his one or two tails in the sophistication of his genius. Oh, I wish I could have a firm good hold of his 1-tailed or his 2-tailed!

It's really no wonder why, when he was such a younger large brain, they had to cut his smart brilliant tail or tails, for if they cajoled him to stay much much longer, they would have ended in obsolescence much much earlier, what with both polyglot and polymath in his two tails [a man of extraordinary genius in letters, and a man of revolutionary science and many more, not to forget what's larger than the atom: his humor!

But of course, God is much ahead of him in humouring his creation, for GOD, THE FATHER, is the greater humourist than MAESTRO ERIMAKO. Did not the Father create a woman out of the ribs of the sleeping man? Didn't He create the universe in just six days, with all the landscaping, the agriculture, engineering, architecture, etc. etc, etc., and he rested on the seventh day? Didn't He save only Abraham, his kin, and their zoo, of a pair of chic and mate, on their large boat, and drowned all of the Earth? Didn't His favoured Moses ride happily on that basket of reeds in the Nile, while the rest of the babes were massacred, found and raised by the Pharoah's sister, then when he becomes a man, drowns the whole of Egypt? How about the head of my favorite, John the Baptist, put on a plate after the Persian danced and gyrated a La Bamba? Well, how about another of His favorites, David, who killed Goliath with just slinging the pebble to his forehead and he sank to oblivion like the Titanic? But, is there anything more humorous than God putting Joshue inside the fish belly, and Joshue kneels to pray? Well, everything is in the Holy Bible, and these stories of evidence show how God loves humor and humouring the faithful. I hope I get the humor of God in the right sense. Oh, Sir Ed now finishes his hot bowl of arroz caldo. I am tempted to ask him: "Sir, which came first, the egg or the chicken?" But I just leave the cliché of heuristics alone as I don't see anymore chicken in his bowl neither the egg, and knowing my professor, he gets more naughty and sexier in mind with the human chic and her ovum. However, I notice that he is more careful with the madness of his exceptional humor because the ears of my twelve-year old seem to be getting bigger and bigger. He teases him from time to time but he does not forget that JP is still a child [only the recent law forgets!]. He then talks of his grandchildren, particularly of Mikaela, the eldest, who does not only excel in Math and Science but also in taekwondo, proof of which is her being a member of the Philippine National Team, Cadet Division. He even accompanies her in her competitions and tournaments. Sir Ed is equally proud of Elyssia, who is an excellent gymnast, with all the top medals in gymnastics, from national gymnastics cups, and has likewise competed abroad. She also excels in Math and Science, so does Eunice. Both girls are SEA-DepEd Awardees in Math and Science as well as YES Awardees. The younger ones, still in elementary, Eoghan, Ima, and Leona are following the Alicias' achievements and excellence, especially in the fields of Math and Science. They are getting many medals in those subjects just like their older cousins. In an interview by DZEC, EAGLE Broadcasting Corporation, with Sir Ed on being a grandparent and as well as on the MTBMLE, he spoke of the importance of non-school factors as determinants of student achievement, and he emphasized on the home, the family value system as vital determinants of academic success. He pointed out that the family values have more lasting impact in children, than the cognitive aspect, as values are lifelong, and eventually, more productive as they become patterns of thinking and behaviour. Clearly, Sir Ed is a man of great knowledge and of sound values as well; he knows how important the family is in raising good children with fine character and an excellent mind. The genius recognizes the family as the most basic unit of society with the greatest responsibility in producing the most responsible and able citizens. Definitely, without question, he has set the bar of excellence to his own family, both in mind and character. But, what is most endearing of his traits? He is a doting, loving, supportive "lolo" to all his grandchildren. One time, he sent me a text message saying he just left Mika in her taekwondo tournament as he got hungry waiting for his granddaughter's match. Then he sent me several updates on Mika's winning over her opponents until she got the Bronze in the recently concluded National Women's Martial Arts Festival. Mika got the Gold, in the Bantamweight Division in 2017. Undoubtedly, the Filipino polymath and genius is very much a good and loving family man. To be more expansive and precise, he is very much human, despite the erudition in his head.

Oh I just can't understand much the logo or symbol on its cover, but the calming pastels of the book, "Notes on the History and Philosophy of Scientific Inquiry, c2017" predispose me to appreciate even more the ambiguities in human knowledge; for, if not for these obscurities, then I wouldn't have the privilege to peek into the cerebral organ of my huge professor, and help myself into erratic moments of sublimation, if self-love is not as coy and shameful. In this noteworthy intellectual curvilinear peak of Sir Ed albeit his prolificity and performance never slide down in the passing of time, with his naughty simile of his superior performance as moderating variable to procreation, both history and philosophy are desirable features in the quest for the best scientific explanation of phenomena in the physical world as well-represented in the case, again of commoner Pedro but whose exigencies in life are nonetheless brilliant prototypes for the universal laws of the sciences. While the chapters on ancient mythology, classical philosophy, biblical genealogy, the age of enlightenment and scientific revolution, deduction of *modus ponens* and *modus tollens* for making inferences, as well as statistical and variance partitioning causal inferences are magnificently eloquent, too eloquent for my insipid science, Pedro's case, I believe is the ultimate scientific theory. And whether axiom, theorem, or postulate, I am more than convinced by the validity and reliability of the conclusive evidence offered again--analogous to the satire, wit, and humor of Pedro, the wife-snatching mah-jong player who's stabbed to death by the cuckolded husband, yet Pedro once more didn't mind that he was already dead. In here, where scientific inquiry is illustrated by, of course, scientific procedure as in the hypothesis-testing on birth control by a neophyte scientist with Pedro and his wife as guinea pigs, my professor's madness of a genius is again metamorphosed into a very plausible, novel scientific principle. Pedro sees the greenhorn scholar for the best means of preventing his wife from repeated pregnancy as they already have four children. The trying hard erudite recommends the removal of Pedro's left testicle as he hypothesizes it's where the sperm cells are produced, and so, the all trusting Pedro gives up his left. But his wife gets pregnant even after, so the struggling Newton recommends the removal of Pedro's right testicle, but after which it fails again as his wife gets another pregnancy. This time around the wanna be Einstein arrives at his best scientific explanation for the birth control problem of Pedro, and his wife. The now enlightened scientist says that the problem should have long been resolved if he removed instead the testicles of Pedro's neighbour. Wow! Sir Ed discusses quite or less ambiguously and wittily the eternal ambiguity of scientific theories toward establishing which theory is a greater falsity or falsehood and which eventually brings to light the principle that is closer to truth, and therefore, some scientific progress is achieved over the ages. In my struggling scientific mind, my professor's humor is by far the best explanation for the greatest faux pas in science. His scientific genius is epistemologically incomparable. Oh, JP whispers to me that he loves science and his science teacher, beaming his best as I again study the face of my professor, searching for better lexemes to describe his current EQ or emotional quotient since his IQ deserves no further probing. Of course, I now attempt to apply the fallacy of the best explanation in my own quest for the truth, which details I will recount in my own autobiography, in memory of my late husband. Ah, my professor has not aged at all. I pinch the crisp chicken breast before me, and thank God, it is not so costly unlike the many celebrated scientific truths. This sexy afternoon is indeed getting even much sexier. And, I'm feeling uncomfortably hot! Maybe the airconditioning is not working well, or perhaps, I got the high fever!

Before I forget my professor's EQ, it is definitely sizzling, scintillating, and statistically trending, that is, nontrivial and significant where Sir Ed's happiness [X], and Sir Ed's contentment [Y] are mediated by his exceptional humor [Z]. Forever a fan of my brilliant professor, I siphon bashfully the *gulaman* in my cold glass of sweet *sago*, while those emperor's eyes watch in esoteric amusement. Oh, it's dusk now, but the sage and the fool continue to converse in the phantom and specter of time. Just like Pedro, they do not mind the impendent horrors of darkness, for as long as books are written and read. JP doesn't mind the dark too for as long as he has computer games to play and that space shuttle to draw. Oh, these three heads must be infuriating Hades for taking the day's burden as rhapsody of the Max's bowl and combo of redundant two.

Now finally out in the market! "The Epigone's Two Cents Versus The Beacon's Five Cents, c2019." The original manuscript was in black and white, reminding me of my small old SONY, black and white TV which my late husband gifted me more than two decades ago. The book's cover now is in three colors; yellow-orange, light blue, and white, with the lighthouse and a ground telescope as main features. Well, attempting again to sound erudite, I believe this book is where my nickel counts: I am what I am, and my professor is what he is. I guess this is in consonance with Aristotle's Identity Principle: A is A. The book is spectacularly brilliant yet very honest, that while it presents counter-arguments to the likewise raised counter-arguments of known and obsessive skeptics, cynics, and postmodernists who always doubt even themselves, the resplendent truth the book offers, in my humble understanding of just four neurons, is that there exists an absolute good, no matter the attempts to disprove and refute its existence. A Higher Being that has gifted the homo sapiens with the faculty of intellect to reason, reflect, and discern is responsible for the creation of the universe, despite the Singularity Theory of an expanding universe. As Sir Ed seems to convey in the book that established science by the famous scientists and minds may be erroneous or false, that these authorities may have erred [like the lighthouse as vanguard of light to the sea voyagers may not be as reliable or no longer as trustworthy], and that new novel vista or perspective of looking at scientific phenomena may be more reliable though unpopular, and the scientist not necessarily as famous [akin to a ground telescope vis–a–vis the towering greatness of a lighthouse]. Well, to me, Sir Ed's point of view means more for the truth in each one of us begins from our own personal experience, direct or vicarious, rather than indoctrinated or as imposed by dogma. But it's always better to check the thesis with an anti-thesis, which should not stop there but should lead to a critical reflection and synthesis. Again, to me, Sir Ed takes the path and inspiration of the TRUE LIGHT, for he is relentless and determined to seek what is true, what benefits mankind. He perseveres to re-examine, re-evaluate existing principles and laws for there might be something even more true than all these. While Sir Ed had first-hand experiences of the supernatural [the first of which was with a black boar following him almost midnight when the world was covered in appaling darkness as the moon seemed to have gone hiding out of fear from some horrific horrendous creature, like the ugly beast in the Irish Yeats's "Second Coming," this frightful-looking four-legged being seemingly trailing, following the young Eduardo, who was around sixteen at the time, sending him to mercurial speed, as he made the Olympic run for his precious life, from the historic Plaza Burgos to their family house in San Julian Sur!

The second encounter of the other world was around 1983 or 1984, with a huge black cat which had burning eyes jumping into their sala from somewhere at midnight and stared at him like the devil; soon after, his wife, Ma'am Teresita fell very ill! And this extraordinary ominous event happened before he boarded the jet for London, wherein he succumbed to much temptation of the flesh, the hours, weeks, months, and years of his falling into the trap of the Prince of Darkness.], he was steadfast with his faith, his convictions, his commitment to carry the torch of life where darkness looms. His science and his spirit kept him marching towards the radiance of the TRUE LIFE. Alluding to Moses and how he was also cast into hell, into the wilderness, into desolation when he killed the Egyptian who wanted to rape a helpless Israelite woman, but his heart and faith put him back to his holy mission of leading the chosen people to Canaan, the Promised Land in which, they went through a lot before they could even reach it. Moses didn't even set foot into this holy land, but just saw it on a hill from a distance until he died. But the beautiful wisdom inspired by this Biblical phenomenon is the faith of Moses and the rest of the faithful in the promise or word of God, which is the truth. So they persevered, and in so doing, they lived with purpose and meaning. While Sir Ed claims to be a nominal Catholic, and that he is skeptical of the resurrection of Jesus, and the Holy Trinity, his ways and his heart speak of his strong faith in God as he prays solemnly, like when I giggled at the middle of my prayer for missing some words but he kept still and reverent of the grace before the meal, encourages me to move on and be strong in the face of my greatest adversity, texts me words of genuine hope, concern, and compassion, as well as lives a happy, productive life as he has always struggled and persevered for, since he was a poor young boy dreaming while he tilled the land under the scourging and scorching heat of the sun. While he writes in his book that "the absence of evidence is not evidence of its absence", to me, this claim is both an understatement and overstatement of his belief for a God who may not be directly visible as when He was a man in Jesus of Nazareth but this God lives in many forms and which remain subject of further probing by scientists. The fact that Sir Ed loves facts as he says, "I beef up my arguments with bits and pieces of evidence, aliunde," and that he even works as a *de facto* lawyer, and excelling in it, his words and deeds are very much of a man, not just of great science but of faith, for yet again, "to love God is to know Him" and the science and ways of Sir Ed lead to what is true, no matter how his humor makes flowers too shy to blush in May or in springtime, or sends virgins washing themselves in no time in stunned lakes and gracious rivers while shrivelled leaves curse time for stealing away their glorious moments in the sun.

On 14 February 2019, he sent me this text message: "I was writing a Motion for Resolution/Judgment on the Pleadings for a legal client the whole Valentine's Day…until midnight. Among others, I used the doctrine, *res ipsa loquitur.*" The man is indefatigable as he continues to sharpen his skills, hone and nurture even more his many talents, indeed, a lifelong learner, in the words of Christian Pastor Lapid in his radio program, "Day By Day."

"OPEN THOU MINE EYES, THAT I MAY BEHOLD WONDROUS THINGS OUT OF THY LAW" [GIMEL Z:18].

There is no question that Sir Ed is a Filipino polymath, maybe misunderstood by some for his genius is inter-atomic, too overwhelming to the short of sight or slothful; his other face of human nature is just too horrendously wicked, hence, many just prefer to shield themselves from its inevitable truth, they fake it, and thus hypocrisy is the overbearing, superfluous face of their humanity. And for this reason, Sir Ed is indubitably, a cut above the rest. He is the new Renaissance Man of the 21st Century!

"I'm lazy to brew my coffee, but I do drink coffee." He tells me before Valentine's Day that the best times to drink coffee, according to recent research are from 9:30AM to 11:30 AM, and from 1:30PM to 5:30PM. Oh, how gracious is this great thinker who continues to go for more light in this universe. "Einstein, did not believe that there's a cosmological constant… his theory of relativity says it so. And this is the greatest blunder of Einstein! He realized his mistake in 1937." Sir Ed once more talks above my head as he finishes his bowl of *arroz caldo* while my son, JP, draws nearer as he gets excited with the genius' instant lecture on the phenomenon of an expanding universe to explain the concept of primordial singularity, as probable origin of everything [of the universe], but, well, I try to raise my counter–argument on the musings of my faith. Since age three, JP, has always loved to sketch and draw of spaceships and space shuttles to bring us to other planets. So, as Sir Ed discourses on all these scientific principles, equations, and probabilities, my twelve year-old's ears get bigger and bigger, making him detach from his computer games. How the genius in Sir Ed captures and captivates the millennial's psyche and interest! Real impressive trait of an erudite to excite, stimulate, and engage even a child in his scientific probity. "Oh, if I just had him as my Science teacher in elementary, I would not have gone missing in the classroom, picking wild flowers behind the bust of Rizal, and chasing the biggest dragonflies in the open fields, wading through the most beautiful sparkling stream behind BANAOANG ELEMENTARY SCHOOL after the heavy rains, rolling my eyes in the marvel of pure, gracious, little, heavenly springs adorning the majestic mountain of my childhood, the legendary, SLEEPING BEAUTY, filling my ears as well with the cheerful laughter and mirth of innocent, pristine, friendly brooks, and if he were my Geometry and Physics teacher in high school, I would not have put up so many excuses to the school doctor so I could ride the *calesa* alone and tour Ciudad Fernandina repeatedly and endlessly, with youthful rebellion and vagrancy in my growing poesy in those times of gentle rains, affable laughter, abundant sunshine, harmless frolic, and carefree of spirit." My sentimental, discerning neuron muses. Indeed, how spectacularly liberating to be so guided, mentored, and inspired through the years by such beautiful mind, much fascinating than the Hollywood film of Crowe. While progressivist education puts premium on enabling the learner to learn how to learn, still the critical role of a mentor on how to make that happen remains.

Intelligence is a gift, no one disputes this fact, especially that in this times and age, a lot of education and social science research as well as pedagogical excitement focus on multiple intelligences and learning styles. Sir Ed, almost, if not, excels in all of these. While brilliance or erudition can be used to mislead, distort, and bring doomsday to mankind, Sir Ed's gifts have been more or less harnessed and used to usher in more light in the various disciplines, never to foil the advancement of human knowledge, much more, with the best of intentions: progress, development, improvement, dynamism, enlightenment. His humor? Just let it be, for humor is the life saver of ennui, misery, and emptiness.

"Yes, most likely he will respond positively! We hope and pray!" Sir Ed boasts my sagging morale one afternoon as I sip my coffee in anxious wait and uncertainty of my print's fate. The man is full of positivity; so, why doubt his faith? He, himself is the living testimony of a ravishing robust faith in one Supreme Being. His patience with me, with my being rogue and folly, with my sluggard typing and staccato vagrant work ethic, with my temperament and grief, with my dumbness and bluntness, with my schizophrenia and scandal, my professor just patiently and graciously waits, listens, and banters with my being a bandit. He teases my despair: "Yes…record waiting…"

Though it has just been barely two months that I've gotten more intimate to the great mind of my professor since 1984 [after 35 years!], I am now in much greater awe and respect, for I see in the brilliant and poetic contradictions of his mind and heart, LIFE IN FULL SWING. He is not frightened by darkness, he takes his steps further, makes giant strides towards the light, so that you and me, ALL OF US, will know more, will see more, and will live more.

Truly, the mark of a great scholar, he believes in knowing the truth. His genuine faith radiates through his diligent, dedicated, selfless works. I'm more than impressed and touched, immensely inspired by his strong will to continue living his dreams, the dreams of his childhood, the beautiful life he desired, to rise from misery and poverty, to seek relentlessly for the answers of life's basic math, the fundamentals of sleep and rousing, to decipher the distances of the basic institutions of society, to learn to laugh with both the little and big jokes of life, the marvel of life and death; and, as he anticipates the publication of his latest masterpiece, his latest *obra*, he enjoys a cold can of Pale Pilsen, with the contentment of a sunset that has cast its magical greatness upon a world too deliriously stunned to pay homage while the dusk puts the gracious glow on the fine gray of the genius.

"Ok, let me recall more anecdotes or episodes. Mistakes? Mistakes in life? I don't regret how life has unfolded in my case, it's the Hand of Destiny that gave me what and who I am now! I have had good breaks, as well as bad breaks, indeed heartbreaks in life, but that is life here on earth. What is important is that in every trying circumstance I did my best to surmount the same, to turn it into one great positive opportunity for achievement, performance. On the whole, on hindsight life so far has given me a net positive balance, and hopefully it will in my remaining years of life. Like the song by the Abba Group/Sisters, I say: If I had to do it again, I would, Fernando."

EDUARDO REZONABLE ALICIAS JR.
"I am romantic empiricist laced with a lot of humor."
------ERIMAKO------

PART SIX
SERENDIPITY

Blazing Light

"*Mama, bayad po!*" I extend my unsure hand to the other commuter near the UP Ikot driver. A confident curly head turns to my direction. Oh, he's my professor in my first class on the first day of AY 1984-1985, Dr. Alicias. I keep my floral covered notebook safely tucked in my likewise floral bag. He smiles a little, then he forgets about the twenty-year old.

"Hi Sir! How are you *po*?" Sir Ed is in a hurry to his class so am I. "Emely, they like you much in the Language Department." Sir Ed tells me. This was in the early nineties. We bumped into each other at the Benitez Hall Lobby, College of Education, UP-Diliman.

"Oh Sir, are you waiting for someone?" I ask the intellectual-looking man in ordinary clothes, standing at a corner near the UP International Center. I just tutored Jeong Won, a Korean M.A. Language Teaching student. "I'm just waiting for a ride." Dr. Alicias smiles at me but he then turns to an approaching man, the dashing Lorenzo Quiambao Orillos, his colleague at the College of Education. "Oh, Lorenz, *kumusta*?" He chats with my boyfriend then, and again, he forgets about the now thirty-one year old former student of his. This was in the mid-90's.

"Do you have a ride, Sir? I offer my newly bought second hand red Hyundai sedan as I step on the brakes for my former professor at the Department of Educational Administration. He points to another car, waiting handsomely to the driver-owner. I then step on the accelerator a little more consciously as he waves and turns his back, proceeding to the old UP Shopping Center. This was sometime late 90's.

"Would you write my Recommendation Letter, Sir?" I ask him coyly as I squeeze the nice muscle of Lorenz on his left arm. Sir ED looks at me rather pensively, and nods his head. Oh, I feel relieved that he is not at the very least an Eskimo, as that would mean a big "NO!" The two gentlemen, but with more noticeable fine gray on their manes, talk a bit. The mood is somewhat pallid but I just silently wait, a nd when the two former UP colleagues shake hands quite firmly with a look of sadness in their eyes, my sneakers hesistantly move down the UP Bliss Housing, saying my faint "Goodbye, Sir!" to the professor who made me blush and laugh, laugh and blush on my first day of graduate class in the country's top university. This was around 2003.

My three UP female professors wanted me to teach at the UP College of Education in that same year, 2003, that was why I needed the recommendation of Sir Ed. One told me to apply at the Department of Educational Administration where I earned my M.Ed., the other two, they instructed me to forward my application at the Department of Language Teaching where I finished my PhD. I almost had two simultaneous panel interviews with some of the country's most eccentric and colourful intellectuals. The younger sister of the late Senator Miriam Defensor-Santiago was very nice, and she asked me which department I liked better. I replied [Of course, I still remember!]: "Frankly ma'am, I'm presently teaching in ADMU, but sure, I love UP because I studied here. Dr. Eliza Paqueo-Arreza actually told me to apply here. I guess I was pushing my grocery cart in Shoppersville when I bumped into her. Oh, I told her I might not be able to teach the way my idol old professors did in the department, and such shame. However, she insisted so I'm here today." Dr. Nene Santiago got curious. She urged me on. "Well, Dr. Alfonso Pacquing was a dynamite! He taught us that the best educational leadership and management style is, I'll scratch yours, you scratch mine! With Dr. Arreza, she strongly emphasized in our Ethics of Education class not to spell her maiden name with a "C" [Dr. Pacquing's!]. Dr. Balmores, wow! He spoke above my head while he burned my lungs with his chainsmoking as I was seated next to his royalty, the King's man. He spoke in fluent but difficult English as most of his words were high fallutin, I could not even find them in Oxford and Webster. Dr. Guillermo? Oh, so fatherly he'd give me his *baon* as I was so thin and frail and the baby of the Curriculum and Evaluation class. But you know Ma'am, I really miss the most Sir Ed as he kept me laughing all throughout the sem, with all the eggplants, magician balls, sex education, creation, procreation and everything in our Education and National Development class. However, I forgot to talk with sense and recite. I was just scribbling my notes and doing my doodles, wondering if he was an immortal from Mt. Olympus, so brilliant yet so erotic and lustful in speech! Well, not to forget, so sexy and handsome! I was twenty, Ma'am and so, I fantasized of him a lot! But, he liked all the voluptuous and beautiful principals, coordinators, and university officials. I just had him in my dreams! Well, Ma'am, that's all I can say today. Thank you for the wonderful question." The Senator's sister then informed me there was no course yet they could give me that semester.

Oh, I later realized while walking past the Oblation that I didn't answer the question of the Senator's sister. Neither did I get the slot in the other Department because a poison letter was sent to the Dean then of the college that Professor Orillos was my boyfriend. Maybe the letter sender was jealous or envious, the crab mentality culture, or the moral standards at the time were just too high, I failed to fit in. But anyway, I was happily teaching the Ateneans "Fiction and Poetry" at this time, with those blue eagles shocking and amazing me with how they would interpret Blake's "The Sick Rose," Dumdum's "Mayon Volcano," Rufo's "Because We Are So Poor," Frost's "Desert Places," Maupassant's "The Jewels," Joyce's "Boardinghouse," Hesse's "Sidhartha" and many more. I learned the wisdom of being resourceful and prepared at the crossroads from my genius professor, Dr. Eduardo R. Alicias Jr. who would always espouse a pragmatic, workable, effective game plan---always looking for opportunities and possibilities. The Pragmatist, the Empiricist, and of course, the Romanticist.

Years, Years. And More Years.

OCTOBER 2018. Unexpected reunion of the erudite professor and the now widow of the late Professor Lorenzo Quiambao Orillos. Over Facebook. She just discovered of her little book, "75 YEARS OF JOURNEYING IN GOD'S GRACE" in Google. Then her old UP professor's name and face blinked on the screen. Serendipitous?

DECEMBER 2018. Widow and son fail to pick him up on time at the façade of historic Vigan Cathedral, but he waited for almost two hours; thus, he left for home the holy place with then unfinished cobblestoned pathways around the church and the city, with a prompt text message to just proceed to San Julian Sur, Vigan, where his estate is. However, the now embarrassed widow just had a zooming blood pressure which explains for the tardiness to meet her genius professor to bring him to her husband's tomb. Prior to the high BP, widow's hands were full, cleaning the house, preparing the table, checking the curtains, feeding the zoo, and wiping her tears with her old floral apron as she cleared her Lorenzo's black and maroon granite tomb from the fallen dried mango leaves of the loyal sentinels that surround the eternal rest of her one and only GREAT TRUE LOVE, robbed from her by the cruel merciless cold scalpel.

JANUARY 2019. The lowly inconnu author of a little world seller offers to write the biography of the author of a Guinness World Record book. He then agrees, and entrusts on his former UP student, whom he gave the lowest grade of the class in 1984, his whole life. The contract was made and witnessed by a bowl of blushing tuna and two plates of crispy fried chicken, one juicy breast, and one sexy thigh, perfect for the world's sexiest mind.

SERENDIPITY???

These are but the wiles of a woman; may I indulge you!
He studied at Divine Word College in Vigan.
She went to St. Paul College, Vigan.
Just a stone's throw away.
He went walking on his *bakya* or slippers to a public school.
She did the same though it seemed she had more time to frolic in the sun.
He was born in Cabuloan, Sta Catalina, Ilocos Sur.
She was born at home, in Santa, Ilocos Sur.
Revolutionary he has been.
Rebellious she has always been.
Both went to UP to see the Oblation and shout, SINO KUNG HINDI TAYO, KAILAN KUNG HINDI NGAYON!

He taught near and far with his humor.
She taught everywhere with her principle.
He married his Chemistry Professor.
She married her Linguistics Professor.
His birthday is August 10, 1945.
Her late husband's birthday was August 10, 1947.

NOT MUCH OF SERENDIPITY?

His star is so big, and shines so bright!
He continues blazing the trail.
She struggles to trek her own though lonely road.
Her dog, Linda Cassopeia gives her the magic of the stars.

As her Lorenzo and their little JP would push the grocery carts, she was behind the lazy steering wheel, reading, "Tuesdays With Morrie"; her Lorenzo dies from cruel hands, now she meets on Saturdays with Alicias, to write his biography, her then professor in UP.

When was the last time she wrote the biography of a 75 year-old man of faith? That's the world seller, "75 YEARS OF JOURNEYING IN GOD'S GRACE." She wrote[as co-author] it with her tears upon the death of her beloved older sister. That was after a year of her MANANG ERLEEN'S death in 2005.

Now, she's writing again but the biography of a 73-year-old man of science. She writes and chronicles the life story of the only living Filipino polymath, again with her tears with the tragic death of her husband, her one and only true love. Her beloved Lorenz died in 2017, a year after, she reunites with her old professor to write of his life.

SERENDIPITY OR NOT,

But destiny meant for two old paths to once more intersect.
What for, and for what?
So, for one life to be written.
So, for the other to exist again.
So, for many more lives to cross and intersect.
TO GLORIFY THE GIVER OF LIFE.
HIS GOD. HER GOD. OUR GOD. AMEN.
THE SANCTIFICATION OF SINNERS, THE GLORY OF
SCIENCE, THE GLORY OF FAITH. E. ALICIAS, JR.; E.
BATIN-ORILLOS;THE PROFESSOR, THE STUDENT.

BLAZING LIGHT
…in the Grace Of
One Journey!
EMELY BATIN-ORILLOS
MARCH 2019

ADDENDUM A POSTERIORI

KEEP YOUR EYES
ON THE BLAZING LIGHT!

IT'S GETTING SEXIER!

EPILOGUE

AN ODE FOR ERIMAKO
MY PROFESSOR

When I was young and dumb
When life was still but pleasant
When learning was full of excitement and dreams
You, MAESTRO ERIMAKO inspired me to be and become.
While the years brought the tears
While the years took away the fun and the bliss
While the years saw you weep
You, MAESTRO ERIMAKO still reaped.
They, who didn't know you well, judged you
They, who were threatened by your luster,
ganged up on you
They, who didn't know any better, persecuted you
You, MAESTRO ERIMAKO weathered all the storms.
For all that has been, good or bad
For everything that was sacrificed, dream or affluence
For time that was spent or lost
You, MAESTRO ERIMAKO fought your best.
Each life is unique. Each life has its mystery and magic.
You lived your life to the fullest for your children to
live theirs.

You did not give up from all the ordeals and trials.
You, MAESTRO ERIMAKO made a father's supreme
sacrifice.
Few of the best minds are gracious with patience
Seldom are the scholars who'd bear with mistakes
Many are just too busy with their erudition, they forget
their family, worst they abandon them
You, MAESTRO ERIMAKO took it upon your
responsibility
Not just to fend for your family
But also for humanity.
Thank you, for all the lessons, the learning,
and the fun
Thank you, for all the books and the wisdom
Thank you for sharing with me and the world
Your life and your light
You, MAESTRO ERIMAKO
…The lamp in a forgotten street
…The candle of a widow and her fatherless child
…The radiant light in the dark, A BLAZING LIGHT!

CUL DE SAC

WHERE & WHEN THE
SPERM MEETS OVUM

Nothing matches the privilege to have been mentored by the Father and the Genius of a GUINNESS WORLD RECORD book, "Humor and Madness" [c1997], and an equally extraordinary *obra*, "Humor and Madness, Jr."[c2009], aside from all his other invaluable writings and achievements, for the inspiration and imprint of his greatness can never be ignored, neither wasted nor set aside. While it's true that I was young and naïve, the first time we met, the seeds of self-fufillment were then searching for where they could grow, that one day, that young woman will also find her own little comfortable nook in this world. And while I've lost contact with my professor for thirty-five years, these almost two months of close and intimate conversations and discourses with him just compensated for the lost times of learning more and getting inspired further from and by him; his principles, his convictions, his knowledge, his wisdom, his life. When he agreed for me to write his biography, I thought he was just a genius as the years brought us apart, going our own ways, living our own lives. He was my professor so I have always known of the man's brilliance, well, even his very green mind. But

I never realized that such a man of great knowledge, of such fabulous and stellar achievements can be so well-grounded, so humble, so patient and kind, so warm, thoughtful, and loving; yet, firm with his principles. He was very patient with my almost a month's encoding of my own manuscript for this served as my very first time to print my own book before it went to the publisher. It seemed much easier to draft the book, which took me a whole month than to encode or print, with my very infantile computer literacy, having always preferred my little pen and notebook for their sacred privacy. I am forever indebted to such a rare Filipino genius. For the trust and confidence he accorded me, I can never forget the golden moment when he said, "YES!" That was the time the ovum found life again in the womb of mortality. The great sperm indeed is a harbinger of better times and better things to come. Why condemn the sperm when the ovum needs it to live? Isn't life become more wonderful and meaningful when the sperm and the ovum build a fellowship so that human life continues, regardless of whether they will one day come to an end? I believe the universe began with the sperm of life [desire to live] and proliferated with the willingness to co-exist [the ovum]. God, the Father has always been around in time and space; He was just waiting in one zillion of moments which sperm and which ovum were willing to come forth and multiply. Dr. Eduardo Rezonable Alicias, Jr. is a well-deserving sperm that should continue to exist in this universe for many more ova, and yes, many others likewise of sperm to find their reason for existence. The way he has lived his life, from grave sin to his redemption, is very inspiring, indeed, a true story of humanity; his journey, THE TRIUMPH OF THE HUMAN SPIRIT OVER EVIL, is one of grace. His blazing light is a blessing to each and every life that he touches for he, undoubtedly, brings hope [to the confused, lost, and helpless], joy [with his humor], and contentment [for the good example of astounding success through hard work and faith]. Truly, HE IS A JOLLY GOOD FELLOW, A BLAZING LIGHT…in the Grace of One Journey!

And his prayer all these years? "Lord, let me, let us have a safe journey!" "Now also when I am old and grayheaded, O God forsake me not; until I have shewed thy strength unto his generation, and thy power to everyone that is to come" [Psalm 71:18].

--EDUARDO R. ALICIAS JR.

Thank you, Great Sperm, my dear old professor! From one ovum, your former student.

FOR LIFE IS PRECIOUS AND SACRED,

LIVE, DO GOOD, LIKE
EDUARDO R. ALICIAS JR.

BLAZING LIGHT, 2019 [E.B. ORILLOS]

APPENDICES

MY FAMILY

Circa February 2019

EDUARDO R. ALICIAS JR.
Married to **TERESITA S. RAQUEPO**: Bachelor of
Science in Pharmacy, UP-Diliman; Master in Science
Teaching, De La Salle University; retired professor,
University of Northern Philippines

Daughter **LILLIAN R. ALICIAS**: Bachelor of Science in Chemistry, UP-Diliman; Master of Science in Chemistry, UP-Diliman; former chemistry instructor, UP-Diliman, College of Science

Married to **EMMANUEL S. RAMOS**: Bachelor of Science in Chemistry, UP-Diliman; Master of Science in Chemistry, UP-Diliman; Doctor of Philosophy (PhD in Chemistry, New Jersey University; former chemistry professor, UP-Diliman, College of Science; now Department Manager of an American electronics company

Daughter **Mikaela:** senior high school graduating student

Daughter **IRMA R. ALICIAS**: Bachelor of Science in Chemistry, UP-Diliman; Doctor of Medicine, UP-Manila; former chemistry instructor, UP-Diliman College of Science; now radiologist in a number of Metro-Manila medical centers, mainly Pasig Medical City.

Married to **LEONARDO P. VEROY**: Bachelor of Science in Architecture, Technological University of the Philippines

Daughters: **Leona** and **Ima:** elementary school pupils

Son **EUGENE R. ALICIAS**: Bachelor of Science in Electronics and Communications Engineering, Technological University of the Philippines; navigation engineer, Seabed Geosolutions, a multinational oil exploration company

Married to **WILFRA "PINKY" G. GAMILLA**: Bachelor of Science in Human Development and Management, Assumption College/University; project assistant, United Nations Development Programme

Daughters: **Eunice, Elyssia, Eliana** (basic education students/pupil)

Son: **Eoghan:** elementary school pupil

THE SIBLINGS OF DR. ED ALICIAS, JR.

1. DR. ED R. ALICIAS, JR.
2. ROBERT R. ALICIAS
   AB English, Divine Word College, Vigan
   Retired Master Teacher 2, Candon National High School
   Married to Teresa
   Daughter: Myrabeth; **Son**, Robert John

3. CLEOPATRA R. ALICIAS
   AB, Divine Word College, Vigan
   BS Agriculture, Mariano Marcos State University, Batac, Ilocos Norte
   Retired Agriculturist, Department of Agriculture

4. FLORENCE R. ALICIAS
   AB, Saint Paul College of Ilocos Sur, Bantay, Ilocos Sur
   M.A. in Public Administration, University of Northern Philippines, Vigan
   Retired Regional Administrative Officer, Department of Environment and Natural Resources, San Fernando, La Union

5. IMMANUEL R. ALICIAS
   Bachelor of Science in Industrial Education, University of Northern Philippines, Vigan

   Teacher, Vigan East National High School
   Married to: Corazon
   Daughter: Immacor Joy; **Son**: Jordymar

The VPA: As Seen By AURELIO P. RAMOS JR.

So, what is the VPA? If my understanding of the VPA is correct, most probably it is, then it can be schematized in two diagrams as follows:

The pie (chart) represents the total variance of, say, standardized student achievement scores. It is partitioned into three integral parts, namely: the 1st Partition, the variance attributable to the teacher ("teacher variance"; the 2nd Partition, the variance attributable to the "control variables" (non-teacher variables); and the 3rd Partition, the "unexplained or error variance."

Partitions of the Total Variance of the
Criterion or Dependent Variable, e.g.,
Student Achievement Test Scores

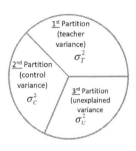

$$\sigma_Y^2$$

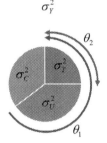

The VPA seeks to infer or indirectly measure, that is, to make the closest feasible estimate of the variance of student achievement scores attributable to the teacher [1st Partition ["teacher variance", *theta*1 (Θ1)]. It is not difficult to see that *theta*1 (Θ1) encompasses any and all observable and unobservable attributes of the teacher—as opposed to the hitherto conventional direct approach of estimating the purported causal effect(s) of a small finite set of teacher attributes on student achievement.

The internal logic and intrinsic beauty of the VPA is that it seeks to minimize the 3rd Partition (unexplained or error variance, squared σ_u) by way or means of maximizing the 2nd Partition (the variance attributable to the control variables, squared σ_C). It is not difficult to see that as the number of control variables approaches infinity, the 2nd Partition (squared σ_C) approaches its maximum value—even as the 3rd Partition (squared σ_U) approaches its lower limit, which is zero (0). Or, equivalently, at infinity, the 3rd Partition (unexplained or error variance, squared σ_U) gets conflated with the 1st Partition ("teacher variance", squared σ_T).

Theta2 (Θ2) is hereby defined as the true or actual measure of teacher variance that occurs only at infinity where and when the 3rd Partition (squared σ_U) coincides and/or gets conflated with the 1st Partition (squared σ_T). Obviously, in real-time and real-life conditions, *theta2* (Θ2) is not amenable to being measured, beyond the reach and realm of direct mensuration, for the obvious reason that infinity is unattainable, unreachable.

Theta1 (Θ1) is defined as the proportional variance attributable to the teacher which is obviously the sum of the 3rd Partition (unexplained or error variance, squared σ_U) and the 1st Partition ["teacher variance", *Theta2* (Θ2), squared σ_T]. It is not difficult to see that *Theta1* (Θ1) is very much amenable to conventional statistical estimation procedures, and this is given by $1 - R^2$ (coefficient of multiple alienation or non-determination) that proceeds from ordinary least squares (OLS) multiple regression analysis where a finite number of control variables are the included and specified regressors. In practice (real-life classroom situation), the number of control variables (regressors) is dictated by the class size or number of students in a particular class.

Offhand, the control variables (regressors) that come to mind, at first blush, are the student's IQ, pretest achievement score (if available), and student's socio-economic variables, etc.

In our last face-to-face discussion on the VPA, I wondered loudly how Dr. Ed ever got to imagine, conceptualize, and formulate the VPA. His short and succinct, emphatic and analeptic answer almost knocked me off my tympanic balance, thus: "Jun, the flash of inspiration favors the naughty, non-Platonic, peripatetic—and, of course, the almost erotic, erotogenic mind." Indeed, this VPA could only have been drafted and crafted by him who can wield the quirks and flourish of "ERIMAKO'S PEN"!

ERIMAKO'S PEN★

Your pen is six inches long and strong.
Its head is big, bald and bold, brainy.
Its nib will write—to right the wrong.
Your pen is it any day, sunny or rainy.

Handled well, it rises to any occasion.
It can trace a concatenation of strokes.
A brainy issue can come out with passion.
It comes alive even with impassive stokes.

Held with fingers of sobriety, propriety;
it will ooze with a lot of rationality.
Fingered with a touch of emotive variety,
it will exude with a cup of seminality.

It is free as the wind is always free,
circumscribed only by a sea of eternity.
It minds not fear nor a proffered fee.
It gets madness into a nest of serenity.

Your pen is six inches long and strong.
It pulses with the beat of a mighty horde.
It is pushed or pulled to right the wrong.
Your pen is mightier that a mighty sword.

Eduardo R. Alicias Jr.
UP-Diliman, Quezon City
October 3, 1997

*This poem is the last portion of the longest preface relative to total book length (world record, **Humor and Madness, c1997, ISBN 971-91402-3-2)**, as recognized in 1999 by the London-based world records organization. This was also published in *Rainstorms and Rainbows*, an anthology published by the International Library of Poetry (ILP, 2000), Owings Mills, MD, USA. It is one of just eleven poems included in the ILP's CD recording entitled: *Sound of Poetry*. Internet surfers can also read this in the ILP's website: *poetry.com*. The following year it likewise appeared in *2001-A Poetic Odyssey*, an anthology published by the *Famous Poets Society* (2001), Talent, Oregon, USA. This was written on October 3, 1997 as Erimako's birthday gift to wife, Teresita.

MULTIPLE REGRESSION ANALYSIS: ITS NOVEL USE IN IMPACT EVALUATION
Eduardo R. Alicias Jr.

Impact evaluation seeks to assess the changes that are directly attributable to a particular intervention such as a policy or program or project. It is usually done to assess the intended changes, and ideally the unintended changes as well. It seeks to determine the causal effect(s) of the intervention, i.e., as to whether or not the intervention has achieved its intended outcome(s). In short, as the term denotes, impact evaluation is in fact *evaluative* in nature; it seeks to evaluate the *effectiveness* of the intervention, in terms of the stated intended outcome(s). This is usually done at the end of an operating cycle (e.g., project cycle), and which findings are to be used to decide whether or not such policy or program or project should be discontinued; or continued as is, or continued with modifications for improvement. To reiterate, impact evaluation is *causal* evaluation, that is, it seeks to inquire whether or not a particular intervention is the probable direct cause of the observed *output(s)* or *outcome(s)*, or even *impact(s)*, qua impact, as some writers would go further.

The best way to do impact evaluation is to do an experiment, i.e., a randomized controlled trial (RCT). However, there are constraints on the use of RCT the most difficult of which is that of constituting random samples of both the control and experimental groups. Thus, it is usually the case that the use of *ex post facto* data is resorted to; and, the best way to analyze the same is to do some kind of a multivariate analysis like multiple regression analysis (MRA).

MRA finds latest important application in the field of educational research, i.e., evaluating teacher performance. My innovative **Variance Partitioning Analysis (VPA)** should be of great utility to educational administrators and principals in their routine effort to objectively evaluate teacher classroom performance. (See related addendum written by Aurelio P. Ramos Jr. on Variance Partitioning Analysis, VPA).

The Holy Grail of Impact Evaluation: The Factual vs. the Counterfactual

The ideal impact evaluation design is to compare a measure of an outcome of an intervention (program or project)—such measure is technically called the *factual*--against a *counterfactual* that indicates what would have happened to beneficiaries or participants had they not experienced said intervention. This design permits the inference that the intervention is *the direct cause* of the observed outcome change which is presumably and expectedly beneficial.

The basic impact evaluation formula can be written as follows:

$$\Delta Y = (Y \mid P = 1) - (Y \mid P = 0)$$

where ΔY = the impact of, say, program **P** on outcome **Y**, and where ΔY is the difference between the outcome Y with the program (i.e., where and when P = 1 {**P$_1$**}) and the same outcome Y without the program (i.e., where and when P = 0, {**P$_0$**}). (Adopted and adapted from Gertler, Paul J., Sebastian Martinez, Patrick Premand, Laura B. Rawlings, Christel M. J. Vermeersch; **Impact Evaluation in Practice**, Washington DC, USA, The World Bank (2011).

It is not difficult to see that, in the aforementioned formula, the term $(Y \mid P = 1)$ represents the *factual*, and the term $(Y \mid P = 0)$ represents the *counterfactual*. In other words, the counterfactual is what the outcome Y would have been at a particular spatio-temporal region--on the part of the intervention or program beneficiaries or participants--had they not experienced the said and the same intervention or program at and on the said and the same particular spatio-temporal region. Now, the impossibility of measuring the non-existent counterfactual should appear obvious to the reader.

Also, it is not difficult to see that this basic impact evaluation formula is valid for anyone or anything that is the unit of observation and/or analysis—e.g., a person, a household, a community, a business organization, a school, a hospital, or any other social unit that can be affected by a particular intervention (policy or program or project). Likewise, the formula is valid for any outcome Y that is conceptualized to be related to the intervention at hand, subject of instant evaluation or analysis. When valid and reliable measures of **P$_1$ (P = 1)**, with intervention (the *factual*) and **P$_0$ (P = 0)**, without intervention, (the *counterfactual*) are gathered and then estimated/analyzed, then it is and should be easy to answer any question about the intervention's impact.

Now, to repeat, this is the ideal design of impact evaluation. That being the case, it is therefore the holy grail, as it were, because both the factual and the counterfactual cannot logically and nomologically coexist at any one point in time and space, since it is obviously the case that someone or something cannot both *be* and *not-be* at and on the same spatio-temporal region. Indeed, measuring two different states of one and the same entity at the same time is impossible. In reference to the aforementioned formula, a person or a thing or a system obviously cannot both be $\mathbf{P_1}$ $\mathbf{(P = 1)}$ and $\mathbf{P_0}$ $\mathbf{(P = 0)}$ at and on the same spatio-temporal region, i.e., at and on the same particular region of spacetime, *pace* Einstein. In short, in the real world, there exists no direct and observable counterfactual; and therefore, as such, its magnitude can only be estimated and approximated. This is the "counterfactual problem."

In this connection, the Asian Development Bank asserts that "the central objective of quantitative impact evaluation is to estimate unobserved counterfactual outcomes" (*Impact evaluation: methodological and operational issues*, Asian Development Bank, September 2006). Likewise, Judy Baker (2000) emphasizes that "determining the counterfactual is at the core of evaluation design" (Baker, Judy; **Evaluating the Impact of Development Projects on Poverty**, The World Bank, 2000).

The Gold Standard of Impact Evaluation: The Randomized Controlled Trial (RCT)

The impact evaluation design that yields the closest and most truthful estimate--i.e., the verisimilitude (*pace* Karl Popper)--of the counterfactual is the randomized controlled trial (RCT). This is the gold standard, as it were, of impact evaluation. In the simplest RCT, there are two groups, namely: the *treatment* or experimental group (those treated with the intervention) and the *control* or ideally the *placebo* group (those not treated with the intervention). The RCT is an experiment conducted in such a way as to minimize or altogether prevent the occurrence of and/or to remove as many biases as possible from the constituent procedures of measurement and comparison, the resultant showing of which is the presumed and probable direct causal effect of the intervention, i.e., the *treatment*. In other words, the resulting difference (see aforementioned Δ) between the treatment and control groups in terms of the outcome $\mathbf{Y}$—if any and if significant—is the verisimilitude of the counterfactual, i.e., theoretically the counterfactual's closest and most truthful estimate.

The RCT, if it has to be the gold standard of impact evaluation, must be invested with two attributes, *sine qua non*, namely: first, both the treatment or experimental group and the control or placebo group must be randomized; and second, the experiment must be "double blind."

Why randomize? Theoretically, the counterfactual problem could be solved by identifying and observing a "perfect clone" of each intervention or program participant, and the set of such perfect clones would constitute the ideal control or placebo group which would then yield the ideal and truthful magnitude of the counterfactual. However, in practice, it is impossible to identify such clones, let alone get them to act as "blind" participants in an experiment whose objective is even unknown to them. This impossibility is punctuated by the fact that even genetically identical twins can exhibit significant psychological and/or behavioral differences.

Although no perfect clones exist at the individual level, two groups of individuals can be made to be "statistical clones" of each other by the process of randomization. If the elements of a population of eligible intervention participants are randomly assigned, say, to each of two groups; and, if each group is sufficiently large, then one is considered to be the statistical clone of the other, i.e., one is statistically indistinguishable from the other. The two groups are statistically identical across all properties—both observable and unobservable (e.g., motivation) as well as the observed and the unobserved—except in respect to the intervention or program. Therefore, in practice, the impact evaluator needs to identify a group of intervention or program participants (the treatment or experimental group) and a group of nonparticipants (the comparison or control group) that are statistically identical, except that one group participates and the other does not; and then thereafter, on comparison, any observed significant outcome difference between the two groups ($\Delta \mathbf{Y}$) must be due to the intervention or program.

If feasible, why should it be "double blind"? It is a desideratum, or where feasible *sine qua non*, in RCT that the members of the intervention or treatment group be not aware that they are involved in an experiment, let alone aware that they constitute the intervention or treatment group. Likewise, it is a desideratum or where feasible *sine qua non*, that the members of the control or comparison or placebo group be not aware of their involvement in an experiment, let alone aware of the fact that they constitute the said control group. This is the first instance of "blindness."

The second instance of desired blindness—or, where feasible, required blindness--is that the evaluators (not necessarily the experimenters themselves) be blind as to which members belong to which group in a particular experiment. Thus, it is desirably the case that external evaluators be requested to do the evaluation and/or the analysis of evaluation data.

This experimental (RCT) attribute of double blindness is important in that it obviates the possible influence of psychological factors on the part of both the experimental participants and the evaluators. For example, if some or all the intervention or treatment participants are aware that they are such, then they may be motivated to behave or perform unusually to a greater or lesser extent; and the same can be expected to occur in respect to the control or comparison participants. Indeed, the same psychological phenomenon can also happen on the part of the experimenter-evaluators.

Thus, it is desirable, or where feasible, it is necessary for the experiment (RCT) to be double blind.

REGRESSION DESIGNS

Regression Discontinuity Design (RDD)

Regression discontinuity design (RDD) is a quasi-experimental design that is appropriately and usually used in the evaluation of a social or educational intervention or program that is directed and delivered to a target or eligible population. **RDD** differs from RCT in that in the former there is no random assignment of cases to the intervention or treatment group and to the comparison or control group. Of course, randomization is the hallmark of the RCT design.

He who is eligible to enroll in such a social/educational program is he (*he* embraces *she*) who is at or below/above a policy-determined threshold or cutoff score on a continuous eligibility index--for example, a poverty score ≤ the population 25th percentile point-score to qualify for conditional cash transfer (CCT) benefit or a previous overall scholastic average ≤ 78 to qualify for charge-free government tutoring services.

The basic model of the **RDD** is outlined as follows:

At baseline or when/where there is no intervention or treatment or program (**P**)--at or when/where P = 0, the comparison or control group--the linear relationship between the outcome variable (**Y**) and the continuous eligibility or assignment variable or score (**S**) is given by:

Equation 1: $Y = \alpha + bS + \varepsilon,$

where $\mathbf{Y}$ = outcome variable, α = the constant or intercept term of the regression equation, $\mathbf{b}$ = the regression coefficient of $\mathbf{S}$ (the continuous eligibility or assignment variable), and ϵ = the error term (unexplained variance).

At endline or post-intervention or post-program, or when/where $P = 1$ (the intervention or treatment or program group)—assuming a constant beneficial treatment effect on the part of the treated intervention or program subjects—the aforementioned Equation 1 becomes the regression discontinuity equation appearing as follows:

$$\textbf{Equation 2:} \quad \mathbf{Y} = \alpha + b_1 P + b_2 S + \epsilon,$$

where $\mathbf{Y}$ = the outcome variable, α = the constant term of the regression equation, $\mathbf{b_1}$ = the unstandardized regression coefficient of $\mathbf{P}$ (the intervention or treatment or program dichotomy, i.e., coded $P = 1$ for the treatment or program group; otherwise, coded $P = 0$ for the untreated or control group), $\mathbf{b_2}$ = the unstandardized regression coefficient of $\mathbf{S}$ (the continuous eligibility or assignment scores), and ϵ = the error term (unexplained variance). Take note that the discontinuity occurs at or with the intervention or program variable $\mathbf{P}$, i.e., where there is discontinuity between the P's coded dichotomous variate values $\mathbf{1}$ and $\mathbf{0}$. (For related reading materials, see, e.g., Alicias, Eduardo Jr., R.; "Towards an Improved Analysis of *Ex Post Facto* Evaluation Data: The Econometric Approach;" *Education Quarterly*; Vol. XXXII, No. 1 & 2, January – June 1985: Diliman, Quezon City, College of Education, University of the Philippines; Alicias, Eduardo Jr., R.; "Assessing the Relative Importance of Explanatory Variables," *Education Quarterly*; Vol. XXXIV, No. 1 & 2, January – June 1987: Diliman, Quezon City, College of Education, University of the Philippines; and Alicias, Eduardo Jr., R. "Multiple Regression Analysis," **Educational Research: Instrumentation, Data**

Collection, Analysis; Diliman, Quezon City, UPROBE, College of Education, University of the Philippines, 1994.

Under the **RDD** assumption of constant effect, the slope of the regression line does not change, or theoretically should not change; or, in other words, parallel regression lines are assumed for both intervention and control groups. On the other hand, what does change or can change--if the intervention or treatment or program is in fact effective--is the intercept or constant term that changes from α to $(\alpha + b_1)$ on the part of the intervention or treatment or program group, where b_1 is the constant effect. It is not difficult to see that on the part of the comparison or control group, the equality $(\alpha + b_1) = \alpha$ obtains because of the fact that, in said comparison or control group, b_1 reduces to nullity--given that therein $P = 0$, i.e., that $b_1 P = b_1(0) = 0$; and therefore $(\alpha + b_1) = \alpha$ reduces to $(\alpha + 0) = \alpha$; ergo $\alpha = \alpha$. Hence, the constant effect (b_1) is *per se* the intervention or treatment or program effect, and the statistical significance of which is tested using the 1-tailed test, in view of the theoretically expected positive or beneficial effect of the intervention or treatment or program.

Graphically, this intervention or treatment effect is directly proportional to the jump or drop (vertical separation) of the regression lines at the point of discontinuity or cutoff.

RDD with Multiple Discontinuities

The conceptualization and specification of the **RDD** equation thus far is such that the intervention or treatment or program outcome variable **P** is a dichotomy (2-valued variable, i.e., $P = 1$ otherwise $P = 0$. It is not difficult to see that a multi-categorical or polychotomous **P** can be included and specified in such RDD equation.

Thus, it is not difficult to see that--for example Equation 4, given a 3-category intervention or treatment or program variable, which can be generalized to **n** categories--can be specified as Equation 5 with a polychotomous **P** as follows:

Equation 5: $Y_2 = \alpha + b_{11}P_1 + b_{12}P_2 + b_{13}P_3 + \ldots + b_{1n}P_n + b_2Y_1 + b_3X_3 + b_4X_4 \ldots + b_nX_n + \varepsilon,$

where $b_{11}, b_{12}, b_{13}, \ldots b_{1n}$ are the regression coefficients of the constituent categories of **P**, and where $b_2Y_1, b_3X_3, b_4X_4, \ldots b_nX_n$, and ε are as defined earlier on and hereinabove.

A simple variant of Equation 5—that which is without matching or PSM and sans time-varying covariate(s)—was used by this author, among others and for example, in Chapters 2, 5, 6, and 7 of the instant book. In these studies, the **P**-variable is the "form of government" which was initially scaled or coded as follows: 1 = full presidential, 2 = semi-presidential, 3 = parliamentary republic, 4 = constitutional monarchy, 5 = commonwealth realm [British-type parliamentary form or former member of the British Commonwealth], 6 = semi-constitutional monarchy, 7 = absolute monarchy, 8 = theocracy, 9 = one-party and no-party, 10 = military junta. Then, this scale-type **P**-variable was subsequently transformed or rather sort of disassembled into its constituent and thereafter separate dichotomous categories and resulting in 10 separate independent dummy variables (dichotomous IVs) such that each resultant dichotomous IV was recoded like a typical binary variable, i.e., $P_1 = 1$, otherwise $P_1 = 0$; ... until $P_n = 1$, otherwise $P_n = 0$. (See, e.g., Alicias, Eduardo Jr. R., **Forms of Government and the Occurrence of Coups D'Etat**; Victoria, BC, Canada: Trafford Publishing, 2007).

Avoiding the *Dummy Variable Trap*. Now, in this connection, there is a need on the part of the evaluator to be aware of and therefore not fall into the "dummy variable trap" in specifying the regression equation. Thus, in the aforementioned example, there was a need to drop or not include one dummy variable in the regression equation, otherwise the evaluator would erroneously and disastrously be ensnared into the aforesaid dummy variable trap. And, the erroneous and disastrous consequence of such a trap is the occurrence of a perfect multicollinearity between and among the aforementioned ten (10) spun-off dichotomous or dummy variables (forms of government), if and when all ten (10) of them would be included in the equation; and which perfect multicollinearity would be violative of and contrapuntal to the basic regression assumption that all the specified covariates or co-regressors or IVs must in practice desirably be orthogonal to each other though not necessarily perfectly so, i.e., the IVs must be substantially independent from each other, or, in other words, not significantly correlated with each other regardless of sign.

To drive home the point, consider for example, the IV or regressor variable **sex**, and let it be coded as follows: male = 1, female = 0. The variance embedded this IV variable **sex** is already sufficiently captured between and among the variate values, i.e., between 1 and 0; and quite obviously just this one variable sex is *per se* sufficient as such IV or regressor. And, therefore, there arises no multicollinearity problem. Now, what happens if this variable sex is sort of disassembled into its constituent discrete subcategories, i.e., **male** = 1, otherwise = 0; **female** = 1, otherwise = 0. It is not difficult to see that the information captured and shown by the subcategory/variable **male** is just the mirror image, as it were, of the information captured and shown by the subcategory/variable **female**. This means that in absolute terms (regardless of sign), there occurs a perfect collinearity or correlation between the **male** and the **female** variables. In other words, the correlation coefficient between the said **male** and **female** would be unity (1)—hence, both are perfectly correlated or collinear albeit with opposite signs. Therefore, it would be disastrously erroneous if both **male** and **female** variables were to be included as IVs in the equation. So, it has to be just one or the other to be included and specified as IV in the equation; indeed, just the aforesaid generic variable **sex**.

Necessarily, therefore, one such dummy variable must be dropped or not be included, and in the aforementioned examples, the P_1 (full presidential form) was dropped or not included; and therefore *ipso facto* served as the referent category. This means that all the other nine (9) forms of government had to be assessed as either positively significant (greater than) or negatively significant (less than)--relative to the said referent dummy category (IV), i.e., the excluded full presidential form. (For a related reading material, see for example, Yamane, Taro (1979). **Statistics: An Introductory Analysis, Third Edition**. New York: Harper & Row, Publishers).

Regression Design (RD) with Continuous P-variable

It may be the case where **P** (the primary IV and the focus of evaluation) is not a newly implemented intervention or program; but rather a long-standing social policy or practice or social condition/phenomenon (**P**) and where such **P** is measured instead as a continuous variable—not as a binary variable (dichotomy) nor as a multi-category variable (polychotomy) as previously presented and discussed hereinabove.

If, for example, panel data are involved--say, there is a pre-test covariate or regressor (secondary IV) serving as one among a number of included and specified control variables—then the evaluative regression equation takes the form as shown in the aforementioned Equation 4, except that in this case **P** is continuous, not categorical. The basic variance equation is schematized as follows:

DV (Y) variance = **P** variance + Variance of Control Variables + Error Variance, and which equation is rendered in standard regression notations as follows:

$$\text{Equation 4b:} \quad Y_2 = \alpha + b_1P + b_2Y_1 + b_3X_3 + b_4X_4 \ldots + b_nX_n + \varepsilon,$$

where Y_2 = the outcome variable (a post-test, where panel data are involved), P = the primary IV (the focus or subject of evaluation, a continuous variable), Y_1 = the pre-test serving as a control variable, and X_3, $X_4 \ldots$, X_n = the other control variables, and ε = the error variance.

Now, in the absence of panel data, the evaluative regression equation takes the general form as earlier shown in the aforementioned Equation 3; and where in such a case, P = the continuous primary IV, the focus or subject of evaluation; X_2, X_3 $\ldots$, b_nX_n = the set of control variables, and ε = the error variance.

The Magnitude of Verisimilitude ($\bar{R}^2$): The Desideratum of a Small Quantum of Erratum. The effect of the set of unobserved and/or unobservable factors, given a particular dependent variable (DV), is given by the magnitude of the unexplained or error variance. Now, the unexplained or error variance—after adjusting for the number of degrees of freedom (df)—is given by: **unexplained variance or error variance = 1 − explained variance ($\bar{R}^2$) = 1 − $\bar{R}^2$**. This means, quite intuitively, that the unexplained or error variance is inversely proportional to the explained variance (**adjusted R^2, $\bar{R}^2$**) which is the explanatory power of the specified equation. Also, quite intuitively, it can be seen that a certain specified regression equation is more explanatory than being erroneous if its calculated $\bar{R}^2$ is greater than 0.50—meaning that the unobserved and therefore not directly measured effect of the unobserved and/or unobservable factors which are not included and specified in the equation (the provenance of the unexplained or error variance) weighs much less than that of those factors conceptualized, included, and specified in said equation. In short, such an equation appears more correspondent with and reflective of the state of nature— meaning that it appears invested and cloaked with a greater magnitude of *verisimilitude* (*pace* Karl Popper), even as it appears more ontically and nomologically true. This is the desideratum of having and/or observing a small quantum of erratum.

REFERENCES

Alicias, Eduardo Jr., R.; "Assessing the Relative Importance of Explanatory Variables," *Education Quarterly*; Vol. XXXIV, No. 1 & 2, January – June 1987: Diliman, Quezon City, College of Education, University of the Philippines.

Alicias, Eduardo. R., **Forms of Government and the Occurrence of Coups D'Etat**; Victoria, BC, Canada: Trafford Publishing, 2007.

Alicias, Eduardo Jr., R. "Multiple Regression Analysis," **Educational Research: Instrumentation, Data Collection, Analysis**; Diliman, Quezon City, UPROBE, College of Education, University of the Philippines, 1994.

Alicias, Eduardo Jr., R.; "Towards an Improved Analysis of *Ex Post Facto* Evaluation Data: The Econometric Approach;" *Education Quarterly*, Vol XXXII, No. 1 & 2, January – June 1985; Diliman, Quezon City: College of Education, University of the Philippines.

Baker, Judy; **Evaluating the Impact of Development Projects on Poverty**, The World Bank (2000).

Gertler, Paul J., Sebastian Martinez, Patrick Premand, Laura B. Rawlings, Christel M. J. Vermeersch; **Impact Evaluation in Practice,** Washington DC, USA, The World Bank (2011).

Mills-Scofield, Deborah; "It's not just Semantics: Managing Outcomes vs. Outputs;" retrieved on 27 August 2017 from https://hbr.org/2012/11/it-s-not-just-semantics-managing-outcomes.

"Outline of Principles of Impact Evaluation," retrieved from www.oecd.org/dac/evaluation/dcdndep/37671602.pdf on 8 September 2017.

"Output vs. Outcomes and Why it Matters," retrieved from **Measurement Resources: Achieving Excellence With Data; https://www.measurementresourcesco.com/ouputs-vs-outcomes-matters/** on 26 August 2017.

"Summative Assessment," retrieved on 26 August 2017 from **The Glossary of Education Reform;** https://www.edglossary.org/summative-assessment/.

"Technical Note: Impact Evaluations," retrieved on 8 September 2017 from **USAID: From the American People**,

https://www.usaid.gov/sites/default/files/documents/1870/IE_Technical_Note_2013_0903_Final.pdf.

Yamane, Taro (1979). **Statistics: An Introductory Analysis, Third Edition**. New York: Harper & Row, Publishers.

I MADE A MISTAKE*

Beautiful words
Squirting from
The beautiful,
If not beatified, lips
Of the high and the mighty,
Of the priests and priestesses
Of scholarship and creativity,
And so they appear to be.
Ensconced in the hallowed halls
Of a university yearning
To become and to be—
Bright and beautiful,
To witness the full flowering
Of a bud as yet inchoate.
Beautiful, beautiful words.
I believed them.
I made a mistake.

*This was first published in *Taking Flight*, an anthology published in 2001 by the International Library of Poetry, Owings Mills, MD, USA. Likewise, in the same year, it appeared in *2001-A Poetic Odyssey*, an anthology published by Famous Poets Society, Talent, Oregon, USA. It can also be read in the ILP's website: *poetry.com.*

BEYOND CONTIGUITY⋆

There's so much mystery in your eyes,
so much mystique in your cryptic smile,
so much meaning in your verbal austerity.
I wanted to measure how distant you are,
to divine the meaning of that distance,
to have even only a passing glance,
say, of the outline of your translucence.
I wanted to touch nothing but your pedestal,
to have even only a tangent of contiguity.
I wanted to listen, to plumb, to fathom
the uncanny depths of your silence,
but you are awfully beyond contiguity.

⋆This can also be read in the ILP's website: *poetry.com.*

ABOUT THE AUTHOR

The author, Dr. Emely Batin-Orillos, is a Doctor of Philosophy graduate in Language Education from the University of the Philippines (UP), Diliman, Quezon City. Her doctoral dissertation, "Developing Academic Writing Proficiency and Learner Autonomy" was awarded the Most Outstanding Doctoral Dissertation by the UP College of Education, Diliman, and the Department of Science and Technology in 2000. She has been teaching English, Literature, and Research courses, both in the graduate and undergraduate levels in various colleges and universities in Metro Manila for thirty-five years now. She served as Editor-in-Chief of "SCIENTIA", the Faculty Journal of San Beda College, Mendiola, Manila, for eight years, and as Editorial Associate of a peer-refereed international journal, *KRITIKA KULTURA* of the Ateneo De Manila University where she was an Assistant Professor in its Department of English. Dr. Orillos is Frank T. Villa's co-author of the religious biographical world seller **75 YEARS OF JOURNEYING IN GOD'S GRACE, first printed and published by AUTHORHOUSE, USA,** in 2008. She is the widow of the late UP-Diliman professor, Lorenzo Quiambao Orillos. They have one child, Joseph Mary Peter Paul Lamb "JP" B. Orillos. A special passion of Dr. Orillos aside from writing is taking care of her menagerie[her cats regaled by the queenly, Kitty, and her dog, Linda Cassopeia] as she is truly a pet lover.

Printed in the United States
By Bookmasters